When Will We Get There?

Jenny Austin

First published by Parragon in 2012

Parragon
Queen Street House
4 Queen Street
Bath BA1 1HE, UK
www.parragon.com

Copyright © Parragon Books Ltd 2012
Produced by Instinctive Product Development

ISBN 978-1-4454-6937-9

Printed in China

CONTENTS

PUZZLES AND DRAWING GAMES 118—131

GENERAL KNOWLEDGE AND TRIVIA 132—160

SYMBOLS KEY

 Visual

 Talking

 Number of players

 Age

 Difficulty level

 Face movement

 Timed

 Mystery

 Pen & paper

 MP3 Player

 Action

 Singing

 Quiz

HANDY HINTS AND TIPS

7

Introduction

Any parent who has traveled on a long car trip with children will know that the road ahead is not necessarily a smooth and straight one. Traffic problems aside, the potential for a child or, worse still, several children, becoming bored increases with each passing mile.

When things begin to get a bit cranky in the car, particularly among the children themselves, some form of diversion is needed to restore a little peace and quiet. It is probably better if the diversionary tactic is employed before boredom sets in.

Children usually respond to structured and organized activities, especially when the grown-ups are involved too. Keeping them gainfully occupied with a particular activity tends to divert their excess energy away from causing aggravation or distress to their siblings, or friends, which in turn can raise the stress level in adults. Involvement in an activity can also, in some cases, reduce the likelihood of illness in those prone to car sickness, although the activity should not involve the child in lengthy periods wherein their head is tilted forward and their eyes focused on something within close range, such as reading.

It is hoped that this book will offer some useful activities that will help to make the trip a pleasurable experience for all the family, not just the children! You may need to put your own "inner child's" hat on, but you will be surprised how easily it fits!

Preparing for the Trip

Always assuming that a long car trip doesn't happen at a moment's notice, there are many things that can be done to make the trip a safe and comfortable one. Apart from making sure that the car is prepared for the trip, make some plans beforehand to be sure that the passengers, particularly the children, are catered for, both in mind and in body.

The first priority is to pack the luggage with everything needed at the destination, whether it be a short stay or a long vacation. The next most important thing is to prepare for the trip itself. Apart from obvious things, such as water to drink and a few snacks for along the way, there is an almost endless list of things that will be needed to keep the children occupied and help to stave off boredom. Each of them will have their own favorites that they would like to take along—let them decide for themselves, subject to there being sufficient space onboard.

If left to their own devices, half the contents of their bedroom or toy chest will find its way into the already crowded passenger space inside the car. It is probably best if they are restricted to one or two of their favorites—say two items each. They (or a parent!) will need to make sure that any electronic devices they decide to bring are completely charged beforehand—unless there is a charging device and cable to allow for battery charging en route; a games console or eBook reader is useless when there is no power left in it!

Of course, it will be up to the adults to check all of the above—and to make sure that Mister Flopsy's "friends" don't stowaway when you are not looking; the children will try to outwit their parents on this! Once the kids' own requirements are taken care of, it will be up to a responsible adult (this means you!) to take a more practical view of the things to be taken on the trip. Hopefully, you will have already organized this in advance. The following list of items should jog your memory, in case you may have forgotten something ...

Apart from favorite soft toys for the children (remember, no stowaways!), these items could prove useful: DVDs and CDs; iPods or MP3 players; games consoles and eBook readers (all completely charged!); a good supply of pencils; a lot of paper or drawing pads—preferably some with preprinted squares or graph paper; empty plastic bags for trash; and a "treasure chest" or goody bag with rewards for good behavior or as prizes for the winners of games. Don't forget to take this book too!

With regard to the snacks for the trip, and the contents of the goody bag, spare some thought for the potential mess and debris that these might leave after the kids have enjoyed them. It is also a good idea to bear in mind the possibilities of one or more of the children becoming carsick during the trip; baby-wipes and tissues, together with a sealable plastic bag for them to be put in after use, are also advisable.

Among the games included in this book are some that require the starting time of the trip to be noted and written down. At the end of the trip, the arrival time should also be noted—this is necessary to produce a result in one of the more educational games. There is also a game called Wheel Lottery: with the permission of the owner of the car, the tire is marked in sections with a chalk or nonpermanent marker. Segments are marked off in approximately equal sizes, one for each person in the car, and marked with the name or initial of each passenger: a picture at the back of the book shows the concept. Whether the game carries a prize, or not, is a matter for personal choice, as some could see this as a form of gambling—but it can be played simply for fun. The wheel markings can be checked after the trip, or at each stop along the way, to find the lucky winner.

Before the Games Begin

Before the games begin, establish some ground rules for the trip. Most of these are commonsense items and, if children are not behaving properly, these rules can be read out to them during the trip. Surprisingly, they tend to accept things that are written down and then read out aloud, rather than just being told the same things by a parent.

First and foremost is the concern for the safety and well-being of all onboard. This means that seat belts must be worn at **all** times during the trip. Players should be careful to avoid distracting the driver at any time while the vehicle is in motion or is about to move off. Nobody should do anything that could obstruct the driver's rear view from the mirror in the car.

Before playing any of the games, it should be decided who is to referee any disputes over game results or decisions. Ideally, this would be a person who is not playing a particular game or round, or somebody who will gain no personal benefit from the adjudication. The same thing applies to the appointment of a scorekeeper, unless otherwise decided **before** the start of the game or round.

Have fun with the games and enjoy the trip!

SPOTTING GAMES

I Spy

| | | | 2+ | 3-99 | Easy |

I Spy is probably the simplest, yet most popular, game of all time. It requires only the eyes and voices of the players themselves, and can be used to help pass the time on almost any occasion. This can be at home or on a trip, whether by plane, train, or car. Best of all, it can be played by people of almost any age—so get the adults to join in!

Game play:

Decide who is going to start. That person looks around and silently chooses an object. The other players are given just one clue: "I Spy with my little eye, something beginning with ...," adding the first letter of the object, color, name, etc.; the choice is endless!

Players then take turns to try to guess the object. If they can't give an answer they say "Pass," and the next person has their guess. If all players say "Pass" (or give up!), the chooser has won. If a player guesses correctly, that ends the round, and the lucky winner gets to pick the next "I Spy" object.

Rules:

The chooser must be honest—remember, no cheating—this can ruin the game for everyone! It is a good idea to choose something that is in view for a reasonable period of time—an object that has already been passed, by the time the game starts, should not be chosen. Remember that younger children may have been taught using phonics—they could be starting the object with a "K" instead of a "C"!

Changes

| | 2+ | 3-99 | Easy |

Changes is another simple spotting game, similar to I Spy, that can be played by children and adults of all ages.

Game play:

Choose one person to start. That person looks around the car and tries to remember everything they see. When ready, they close their eyes—no peeking!—while somebody changes the position of something in the car. When done, the player has to open their eyes and try to guess what has been moved. When he or she guesses correctly—or gives up—the next player goes.

Rules:

Try to keep things simple—at first! Choose an object that is visible from where the player is seated, move a sun visor or swap hats, etc. Have fun!

Splat!

2+   5+   Medium

Splat! is a clue-based guessing game that can be adapted to suit almost all ages. In this game, players have to guess the identity of a passing object while the chooser gives a simple clue—the word "Splat."

Game play:

One person picks out an object that is passed frequently on the road. The object can be a bridge, sign, blue car, etc. Each time the car passes the object, the chooser calls out a silly word, such as Splat, while the other players have to try to guess what it is.

The game can be made more difficult by choosing a more specific object, such as a blue sign with a particular word on it. If a guesser is close, the chooser says "Close—but not exact," or something similar. When the object is guessed correctly, that person chooses the next object.

Rules:

Start by choosing fairly common objects, because this helps to get everybody into the spirit of the game. When everybody has had a chance to choose, the next round can be made more difficult by choosing a less frequent or more specific object, such as a car with four people in.

Car Search

| 2+ | 3-99 | Easy |

Car Search is a classic car game that is enjoyed by children of all ages. The game can be adapted to suit the ages of the players and the type of passing traffic.

Game play:

It's best if an adult starts by selecting the type or color of car to be spotted by the players. A good starting point is to pick the car you are traveling in, either the type or the color. The first person to spot a similar car is the winner and gets to choose the next car. There are almost endless variations, including the number of occupants, spotting cars with more than two people in, trucks with words on the side, etc.

Rules:

Keep it simple—don't choose obscure vehicles or colors that are unlikely to be seen!

Tunnel Vision

2+	3-7	Easy

Tunnel Vision is a simple observation game that is particularly suitable for younger children—but anyone can play!

Game play:

A player can play this game with both hands cupped around the eyes to create a tunnel, or by using a piece of rolled-up paper as a make-believe telescope held up to one eye with the other eye closed. The player then looks through the hand tunnel, or the paper tube, and tries to remember what he or she sees over a distance of about one mile or within a short period of time. An older child or adult then asks the spotter if they can remember what has been seen through the tube.

Variation

The player can be asked to give a running commentary of what is seen through the tunnel in real time—this gives an insight into the observation powers of a very young player, as well as being quite entertaining for the other passengers! Asking some trick questions like "Did you see the animal with six legs?" could prove interesting in the replies that follow.

Rules:

Decide how long the game should last. Keep in mind that a child could become dizzy if looking through the tube for too long. When played as a competitive game, restrict the movement of the tube or tunnel to one particular direction—and make sure that the player keeps one eye tightly shut!

The Banana Game

2+   3-99   Easy

The Banana Game is a very easy game to play—but can develop into a very competitive one!

Game play:

First decide the length of the game, either by time, perhaps 30 minutes, or a given distance. A player has to watch out for any yellow vehicle that passes, or is passed. When spotted, they have to call out the word "Banana" to score a point. The winner is the player with the highest score at the end of the time or distance agreed at the start of the game.

As a change from road vehicles, almost any yellow item can be chosen as the Banana. Although the chance of spotting a canary while traveling by car is very limited, remember to call out "Banana" if you do see one because it is worth 100 points!

Variation

Points can be awarded for each type of yellow vehicle spotted. For example, a yellow car is worth 1 point, a yellow truck wins 2 points, a yellow bus could be 3 points, and so on. Don't forget to include a points, value for construction vehicles and cranes!

Rules:

You must call out "Banana" when the yellow object has been spotted—and the object named—before it can be added to the score.

Counting Creatures

1+	3-99	Easy

Counting Creatures is an old favorite that can be played in many different ways. It can be used as a way of passing the time for a single player or as a team game for family play. Easily adaptable, this game can help to pass the most tiresome road trip.

Game play:

The simplest form of the game is for a single player or team to see how many creatures of a particular species (cows, horses, sheep, etc.) they can spot within a given time or distance. If the car passes a school (or any other chosen place or feature), the score is set back to zero, and the count has to start over again. If traveling on a long road or highway, the "home base" can be a rest area, highway service area, or gas station instead of a school. If the car needs gas, every player's score is reset to zero and then everybody has to start over again.

If there is more than one player, the others can take turns at spotting the object over the same time or distance, of around 15 minutes or 10 miles. The remaining "nonspotter" players should keep an eye on how the "spotter" is doing by checking their score—mistakes do happen! Only creatures on the individual player's own side of the car should be counted. If any player is sitting in the middle seat, they have to declare which side of the car they are spotting before the game begins. The winner is the person with the highest number of creatures at the end of the game or trip.

Variation

Instead of creatures, try counting signs, power stations, water towers, or absolutely anything you choose! And remember to select the solitary "home" item before you start!

Rules:

Only the chosen object to be spotted that appears on the player's side of the road may be included in the count. Fingers may be used for keeping score. And remember, the "home" item is unlucky—if seen, the spotter has to start counting creatures all over again!

License Plate Game

1+   5-99   Medium

License Plate Game is a game that will keep the children busy throughout a long car trip. The game requires them to look for cars with license plates from different states.

Game Play:

Make a list of all the states, either before the trip begins or, if preferred, this can be done in the car. It is best that the states are listed in alphabetical order to make it easier to follow. Leave some space next to the list for adding additional information during the game. Just making the list of states will keep the children occupied for some time—and will help reinforce their knowledge of the geography of the country. For checking purposes, a full list of states is shown at the end of this game. When the players' list has been completed—and checked for correctness by a grown-up!—the game can begin.

All of the players then watch out for cars and check off the state that is shown on the license plate against that state on the list. Bear in mind that some states have only one plate—at the rear of the vehicle. The object of the game is to find license plates from all the states on the list. Because it is unlikely that the list will be completed in a short time, it is better to record the date and place that each plate was seen. The name of the first person to spot the plate could also be recorded—this could be of interest when the list is complete to see who has spotted the most states! A further point of interest could be that a tally of plates spotted each day is kept, or a single tally for the total number of plates for the trip—the choice is yours.

California
5SF R185

Louisiana
VSF 460

The game can be played as a points scoring game. A point could be awarded to the person who spots a new, unseen plate from the list. A bonus point is awarded at the end of the day to the person who first spotted the plate from a state that is the furthest distance away from your starting point or home state. Two extra points could be awarded to the first player to spot a license plate from Hawaii, Alaska, or even Mexico and Canada, unless, of course, you live there!

List of the fifty U.S. states in alphabetical order:

Alabama, Alaska, Arizona, Arkansas, California, Colorado, Connecticut, Delaware, District of Columbia, Florida, Georgia, Hawaii, Idaho, Illinois, Indiana, Iowa, Kansas, Kentucky, Louisiana, Maine, Maryland, Massachusetts, Michigan, Minnesota, Mississippi, Missouri, Montana, Nebraska, Nevada, New Hampshire, New Jersey, New Mexico, New York, North Carolina, North Dakota, Ohio, Oklahoma, Oregon, Pennsylvania, Rhode Island, South Carolina, South Dakota, Tennessee, Texas, Utah, Vermont, Virginia, Washington, West Virginia, Wisconsin, Wyoming.

Variation

A variation is to record different versions of state plates. For instance, in Virginia there are Chesapeake, Cardinal, Jamestown, Humane Society, pictures of leaves, plain blue, etc.

Rules:

All claims for spotting a new plate have to be verified by another person in the car. The person who first sees a new state plate gets 2 points and 1 point is given to the first person to spot a new design from any state. Veteran plates score 3 points. A person lucky enough to spot a Medal of Honor recipient plate scores 5 points.

Remember What You Saw

| 2+ | 3-99 | Medium |

Remember What You Saw is an exercise that challenges both the visual and the memorization capabilities of the players taking part. Players have to try to remember objects seen as they travel along a road, then tell the others in the car what they saw.

Game play:

Decide which objects have to be included in the game, because it is almost impossible to remember everything along the road. The objects could be things of a particular color or shape, animals in fields, etc.—the choice is up to the players (or the referee, if there is a difference of opinion!). Set a time limit or distance for each player to have their turn—allow a period no greater than five minutes or so, or a measured distance between highway exits. Try to allow each player the same amount of time or distance.

At a chosen starting point, the player has to try to remember the objects seen and, after the time or distance limit is reached, "time" is called and the fun begins. The player has to remember what has been seen. If, for example, the chosen subject is people, the order they were seen in could be: man, woman, woman, boy, man and woman, girl, etc.

Variation

An in-car variation can also be played. In this version, somebody in the car draws a series of objects on a sheet of paper or notepad while shielding the drawing from the sight of the players. This drawing is then shown to each player, in turn, for a short period—perhaps a count of five, then it is taken from their view. The player then has to try to remember as many of the objects from the drawing as possible. Most objects remembered wins the game.

Scavenger Hunt

2+   3-99   Medium

Scavenger Hunt is another old favorite that all the family can play and enjoy. A list of objects is written on a sheet of paper or notepad; these have to be spotted and checked off as you travel along the road.

Game play:

Before the game starts, as a group decide on a list of objects to be spotted. Each player then writes these down on their own piece of paper. Objects can be as easy, or difficult, to spot as you like—items could include a lamppost, fast food outlet, brown cow, or any other thing you are likely to see on your trip. Younger children should be remembered—so let them have a turn first! (Or give them their own object to spot from the list of things to be found.)

When everybody has checked that they all have the same objects listed, the game can begin. One person chooses a starting point at some distance ahead on the road—this can be after the next overpass, junction or exit, for example. When this point is reached the game begins, and each player has to look for any item on the list. First to spot an object calls out "Brown cow," or whatever he or she has seen that is on the list, and checks it off on their sheet. Other players who may have also seen the object (but did not call it first) will have to wait until they are the first in the car to spot the next brown cow! There is no need to take turns at spotting for objects; each player continues to look

for any of the items on their list. First to check off all of the items on their list is the winner.

When a game has been won, it is a good idea to let the winner choose the next list of objects or, perhaps, choose the next game to play!

Rules:

Before starting the game, be sure that objects on the list can be easily seen from the sitting position of all players, especially smaller children sitting in the back of the car. Items such as a black cat that may be lying asleep in the shade underneath a parked car would not be a reasonable choice for an object. Things that have been claimed as being "spotted" must have also been seen by at least one other person in the car.

Variation

Choose objects of a more specific type—for example, a sign or billboard with a particular word or picture on it ("sale" or "burger", a picture of an animal on a signboard, etc).

Team Challenge: Left or Right

| 2+ | 3-99 | Easy |

Team Challenge is a game to be played by two teams, each with one or more players. The teams take turns at nominating an object to be spotted by their opponents. Younger players can help a team to spot objects even if they can't yet manage to count them, so this game gives the little ones a chance to play along too.

Game play:

Each team represents one side of the car—left or right. It must be decided which team is to be the first to pick an object, and how long each team's turn will last. Game time should not be too long because this will give a better playing experience—five minutes or five miles distance for each team will probably be about right.

The starting team then chooses an object—this should be one that is fairly common, otherwise the game will not flow. The opposing team then has to spot as many of the objects that appear on their side of the car within the given time. When their turn is over, the team that chose the object has then to spot that **same** object, but on **their** side of the car, and within the same time or distance limit. The winner is the team with most objects spotted within the allotted time or distance.

A good playing tip is not to choose too difficult an object—remember, your team will have to spot the same object when it is your turn! Choosing a plane, for example, when you are near an airport, is likely to give an advantage to the first team to play, unless you happen to know that there is another airport coming up soon—and on the other side of the car!

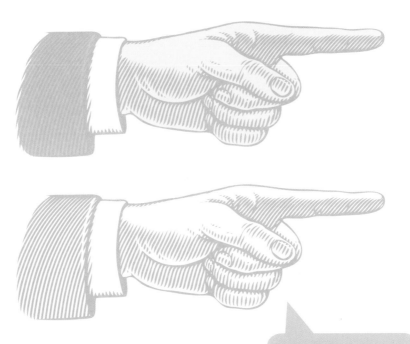

Variation

An object is chosen for both teams to spot at the same time. The winning team at the end of the game gets to choose the object to be spotted in the next game.

Rules:

Because each team takes turns at playing, the opposing team should double-check the objects being counted by the other team. This will ensure that their opponents do not cheat! In the event of a disagreement, the referee in the car should decide whether or not to allow a team's score to stand. If in doubt, the disputed score should return to zero and that team should play again at spotting the same object, over the same time or distance.

Same Car as Our Car

| 1+ | 5-99 | Easy |

Same Car as Our Car is a simple game that can be played by all the family. It is particularly good for those traveling with very young children.

Game play:

The players each have to spot a car of the same make as the vehicle they are traveling in. Each time a car of the same make is spotted, the player who sees it first has to call out "Same as ours" to win a point. The player with the most points at the end of the trip wins.

Variation

Play the game as before, but allow cars of only the **same make and color** to be counted.

Rules:

Only the first person to spot the target vehicle can add it to their score.

Waiting for the Bus

2+   4-99   Easy

Waiting for the Bus is a spotting game that can be fun when driving through a town or city. If there are bus stops on your route, this is the game for you.

Game play:

Two players can play this game, but it's more fun if a team on the left side of the car plays against a team on the right side. Players have to spot how many people are waiting at each bus stop on their side of the road. The person or team with the highest score at the end of the game wins.

Variation

This variation is especially good for busy times in the day. One team or player counts only men, or only women, at the bus stops on their side of the road.

Rules:

Bus stops can only be counted if they are at the side of the road being traveled along—those placed on side streets, or in places not easily visible to the other players in the car, are excluded because these would give one player or team an unfair advantage over the other. People actually on a bus at a stop should not be included.

Subway stations or overhead rail system stops are excluded from this game. Only bus stops are to be included. The referee is to decide whether or not a bus stop is in play or not.

Punch Buggy

2+   5-99   Easy

Punch Buggy is also known as Punch Bug, Slug Bug, or Beetle Bug. This is a game played by children who punch each other on the arm when first sighting a Volkswagen Beetle, at the same time calling out "Punch buggy" or "Slug bug."

Game Play:

The traditional version of the game is based around the original, classic Beetle-shaped Volkswagen. The first person to catch sight of one of these iconic vehicles punches their nearest neighbor on the arm and calls out the color of the car and its type, followed by the words "No punch back" as in the following example: "Red VW Bug sedan—no punch back." If a person fails to say "No punch back," then the recipient of the punch can instead deliver a punch to the caller. Other vehicles from the VW classic range (vans, trucks, camper vans, etc.) may also be included in the game but must be correctly identified and their color included in the call, not forgetting the words "No punch back."

The game can also be played with points awarded for each of the classic VW vehicles correctly identified, according to their type and color:

VW Bug Sedan = 1 Punch

VW Bug Convertible = 2 Punches

VW Van = 2 Punches

VW single or double cab truck = 5 Punches

VW military jeep (very rare!) = 5 Punches

The player with the highest score at the end of the trip, or an agreed time or distance, wins the game.

Punches must be delivered only to the biceps area of the arm! No head, rib, or below the belt punches are allowed. The force of any punch delivered should only be appropriate to the age and physical build of the recipient—NO exceptions!

Rules:

Any type of VW Beetle (or New Beetle) that is located in a place less than one mile from home is not allowed, because any prior knowledge of its location could be considered as unfair to other players. The driver on this trip should not play this game for reasons of road safety but may referee any disputed calls.

Variation

This game can also be played using both the classic VW Beetle and the Volkswagen New Beetle. This variation is played using the same method as for the previous version but with a modified scoring system as follows:

New VW Bug = 1 Punch—New VW Bug Convertible = 1 Punch

Classic VW Bug = 2 Punches—Classic VW Bug Convertible = 3 Punches

VW Van (either style) = 3 Punches—VW single or double cab truck = 5 Punches

VW Thing = 5 Punches

License Plate Alphabet

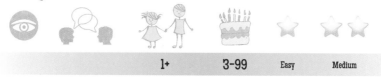

| 1+ | 3-99 | Easy | Medium |

License Plate Alphabet is a simple spotting game for all ages and is based on the letters of a vehicle license plate. This ever-changing source of material should keep even the most bored passenger occupied.

Game Play:

This game can be played individually, with the first player to complete the list or find the most letters in a given time or distance being the winner, or as a team game with all players collectively spotting for letters.

Rules:

The letter "Q," if seen on a plate from the province of Quebec in Canada, is worth an extra bonus point to the first person to spot it.

Alabama

1A23 B45

Make a list of all the letters of the alphabet. Players look out for license plates for states beginning with each letter and write down the name of the state alongside the relevant letter on the list. If desired, "H" (for Hawaii) can be excluded. Any of the listed states can count toward the target alphabet: for example, there are four states beginning with the letter "A," so any one of these states fulfills the requirement for that letter, and so forth. Where no state begins with a particular letter, for example "B," "E," "Y," these letters can be included if seen within the name on the plate from any state, as in "B" appears within the name "Alabama." The letter "Z" is excluded from the game.

List of states:

Alabama, Alaska, Arizona, Arkansas, California, Colorado, Connecticut, Delaware, District of Columbia, Florida, Georgia, Hawaii, Idaho, Illinois, Indiana, Iowa, Kansas, Kentucky, Louisiana, Maine, Maryland, Massachusetts, Michigan, Minnesota, Mississippi, Missouri, Montana, Nebraska, Nevada, New Hampshire, New Jersey, New Mexico, New York, North Carolina, North Dakota, Ohio, Oklahoma, Oregon, Pennsylvania, Rhode Island, South Carolina, South Dakota, Tennessee, Texas, Utah, Vermont, Virginia, Washington, West Virginia, Wisconsin, Wyoming.

Kansas

XYZ 321

New Jersey

BDF 222

Object Alphabet

2+   5-99   Medium

Object Alphabet is a simple and entertaining game for those old enough to know the alphabet and the letters, or sounds, which start the names of objects.

Game play:

Starting with the letter "A," players go through the alphabet while identifying objects outside the car that begin with that letter, for example: Airplane, Bus, and so on. Anybody can call out the letter and object, but it must be visible to all players. Some of the letters can be quite challenging!

A slightly more difficult variation is to restrict the players to using the actual letters of the alphabet itself. These can be spotted on road signs, billboards, license plates, letters on the sides of trucks, or whatever. In this game, the player has to choose both the letter and its source. When spotting the letter "X" on an Exit sign, they have to declare "X on that Exit sign."

Only one letter from any one sign may be used—if a similar sign along the road has another letter that is needed, that sign can be allowed if it is in a separate location from the first sign. Object alphabet can be played by all in the car, or as a team game. The first team to complete their alphabet wins.

Variation

To make the game even more difficult, the source of the letters could be restricted to those spotted at specific locations. This could be license plate numbers on vehicles, street signs, or billboards.

Rules:

Letters and their sources must be clearly visible to all players. A source can be used only once in any one round unless two successive letters appear together on any one source, for example: "N" and "O" on a sign that says "NO PARKING"—but this usage still has to be declared by the player, as before, "N and O on that No Parking sign." A road sign or billboard of the same type can be used more than once—but it must be separate from the first one. This gives an opportunity for some advance planning, but the next letter of the alphabet should not be declared until it is clearly within the sight of all players.

Colors of the Rainbow

1+   4-99   Easy

Colors of the Rainbow can be played by any number of players, either as individuals or as a team game. Please note that this game could be difficult for those who are color-blind.

Game play:

This game involves players in trying to spot objects, both inside and outside the car, that have the same color as those that are present in a rainbow (see the Rules for the colors to be spotted).

Before the game begins, it should be decided whether the colors can be spotted in any order, or which color should be spotted first. The first to spot all of the colors of the rainbow wins the game.

If a player or team actually spots a rainbow in the sky, or a picture of a rainbow on a sign, that instantly wins the game!

In a team game or competition between individuals, first to spot all of the colors of the rainbow wins. If all the colors have not been spotted, the person or team with the greatest number of rainbow colors spotted is the winner.

Variation

As an alternative and much longer game the colors of the rainbow to be spotted may be those of a nominated object. This could be the colors of cars or those appearing on a sign.

Rules:

Only the seven main colors of the rainbow, as seen by a normal human eye, namely those specified by Isaac Newton in the sequence red, orange, yellow, green, blue, indigo, and violet, may be counted. The order of these follows "Roy G. Biv," a useful aid in remembering the colors in a game where the colors must be spotted in a particular sequence. Remember that "violet" is not purple!

WORDS
AND
NUMBERS
GAMES

Sign Language

Animal A to Z

Word Scramble

Alliteration Game

Word Train

Average Speed Game

I Went to the Store

Highway Sign Mayhem

Rhyming Words

Out for the Count

Spelling Bee

Sign Language

1+	9-99	Hard

Sign Language is a game for slightly older children and adults. The game is a brainteaser and requires players to make up other words and phrases from those appearing on signs and billboards along the route being traveled.

Game play:

A person in the car has to choose a word or phrase from a sign or billboard that can be seen by all players. To start with, it is better to choose a fairly simple word or phrase.

Players have to write down that chosen word, place name, or phrase. From that word or phrase, they have to write down another word or phrase using as many of the letters of the original as possible. After a given time or distance, the game stops—then the fun starts. Each player has to read out aloud, in turn, their original word or phrase, followed by their made-up words or phrases.

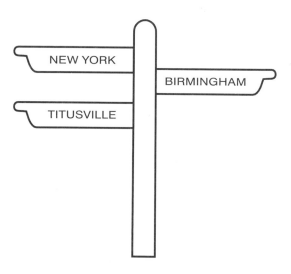

The game can be played as a point-scoring game for individuals or teams of players, using a simple "1 point per letter" method for each word or phrase made from the original. Any leftover letters from the original word or phrase will result in the deduction of 1 point for each letter not used. Letters can only be used the same number of times that they appear in the original word or phrase.

Some example plays are:

1) New York—Keno Wry, Key Worn, Yen Work, Re Wonky, Rye Wonk, Rye Know

2) Birmingham—Bah Rimming, Ham Brim Gin, Ma Bring Him

3) Titusville—Elitist, Vilest, Illusive

4) Burger King—Beg Rung Irk, Burn Egg Irk, Grub Ken Rig

The above examples are anagrams in which **all** of the letters in the original word have been used. Each letter has been used the same number of times that it appears in the original word.

If, in example 4, the player could only make up the word "**bigger**" from the source words "burger king" that would make their score 6 points, but as they did not use the letters "u," "r," "k," and "n," they would lose 1 point for each unused letter (a total of minus 4 points). This would leave their final total at 2 points.

Phrases can be the source of much amusement—and can lead to a large total score for any player who can make up a credible or humorous phrase using most, or all, of the letters from the source billboard:

San Francisco Giants = Fascinating, no scars

Say it with flowers = We flirt so this way

No admittance = Contaminated

Rules:

Almost anything goes (but no bad language or anything mean!). Sensible or silly—they can all score points. You could even have a good laugh at somebody's pathetic attempts. But remember, your own efforts could also become a source of amusement to your fellow players!

Animal A to Z

1+ 6-99 Medium

Animal A to Z is a fun game that is a favorite with those younger children who can read and write the alphabet, and make simple words. It can also be adapted for children of a younger age with support from an older child or adult. If a child is prone to car sickness, the game can be played verbally.

Game play:

Each player has to write down the letters of the alphabet in the form of a list down the left side of a piece of paper (or in columns with sufficient room allowed to write alongside each letter). This gives the younger ones an opportunity to reinforce their schoolwork and is a helpful learning experience.

At the command "Go!" the game starts. Each player has to write down the common name of an animal next to the letter its name begins with, as in C-a-t.

If playing the game verbally with younger children, they can be asked "What's the name of an animal beginning with 'A'" (or its phonic pronunciation, if this is how they are being taught).

Animals that are pictured or have their names written on signs and billboards are allowed. A point is awarded for every animal that is properly named. Double points are awarded for each animal name that is correctly spelled. An extra bonus point is awarded if one of the real, live animals is actually spotted outside the car while the game is being played!

z

zebra

Rules:

A parent or older child should check that all players have written down all 26 letters of the alphabet before the game starts. It should also be decided which letters, if any, should be excluded from the game. The letter "Q" could be the first problem, but "Queen Bee" is allowed. There are at least 25 creatures beginning with "X"—some, if not all, are quite obscure and unlikely to be known by a young child: X-ray tetra (fish) is just one beginning with that letter. Similarly, the letter "U" could be a problem letter—but there is always the possibility of seeing a unicorn!

Word Scramble

1+	9-99	Medium

Word Scramble is a game for the older child—including adults! Parents can decide for themselves whether their children are capable of playing this word puzzle game. Lists of scrambled words and phrases have to be unscrambled to find the answer to the secret code!

Game play:

From the given lists of scrambled words, players have to decipher the words or phrases. Players should write down the name of the game being played and the key letter for the words or phrases to be unscrambled, with their (hopefully) right answer next to the key letter.

For example:

Game X:

a = EPZLUZ (PUZZLE)

b = ALPEP (APPLE)

The solutions should become obvious but (just in case!) answers are given at the back of the book (on page 154). Clue—each game has a different common theme.

Variation

Can also be played with one person creating their own scramble word and everyone else in the car guessing the word.

Rules:

There are none—except NO PEEKING at the answers!

Game 1:
a) ELUB b) GENORA c) WLEOLY d) PRUELP e) ENGRE f) KNIP g) RNOBW
h) KABCL i) IGONID j) TEHWI

Game 2:
a) WCO b) TOGA c) SEPEH d) PTELENAO e) NELATHPE f) RETGI g) RASKH
h) ROPLA ARBE i) DRALPOE j) YNXL

Game 3:
a) JAHELI b) OGREEG c) TRAINM d) MALEAP e) BEDBIE f) EELNIMEDA
g) TINCHISRE h) YEEKEL i) AADMAN j) LANDOD

Game 4:
a) PLUIT b) AYIDS c) HTAINYCH d) LAFDIODF e) HOCDRI
f) MARCHYSUMHENT g) EVILOT h) SORE i) MACAEIL j) PUTBURCET

Game 5:
a) WEN KROY b) DYSEYN c) BRINEL d) MORE e) BAMMIU f) OSA OUPLA
g) SHANJNBRUGEO h) KRNAAA i) OGLETWINLN j) CRACA

Game 6:
a) SINETN b) OCESCR c) TRECCIK d) FLOG e) YEOKCH f) SLABEBLA
g) BYUGR h) HISCALTTE i) TANGSIK j) CGNYLIC

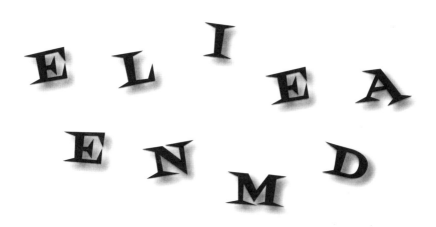

Alliteration Game

2+   5-99   Easy

The **Alliteration Game** sounds as though it could be a complicated or difficult game to play—it is not! This is a very funny game that should amuse all the family, in particular the little ones, who will enjoy making up silly sayings.

Game play:

The object of the game is for the players to take turns at making up alliterative phrases of three words or more, with each word beginning with the same letter of the alphabet. For example:

"Tiny Tommy Taylor" or "Silly Simon Smith"

The game can be played using the first letter of a person's name, or an animal "Gorgeous George Giraffe," or any other object to make up a phrase. Remember to make allowances for the use of phonics by the younger ones—the game still works that way!

Variation

Older children could try making four-word phrases—much more difficult to do, but not impossible, for example: "Big Bad Brown Bear."

Rules:

Just make it up as you go along—almost anything goes, but each word of the phrase must begin with the chosen letter of the alphabet. Be as silly as you like—it's more fun!

Word Train

	1+	7–99	Medium

Word Train is an absorbing game that can be played for fun or as a very competitive team game.

Game play:

Before the game begins a starting word (the locomotive) must be chosen. From this word the players then have to write down a following word that begins with the last letter of the starting word, and so forth. It is a good idea to connect the words of the train together with a dash (—) to represent the couplings of the wagons in the word train.

In the following example, the starting word (locomotive) is pulling three wagons (words):

Locomotive—electric—car—railroad— ?

The word train can be any random sequence of words. As a more difficult variation, it can be themed so each word must follow a particular subject (railroads—as in the example above, animals, people's names, etc.). As a game between individuals or teams, the person or team with the longest "train" (number of words) is the winner of that round and gets to choose the next subject or theme, and the "locomotive" word.

Variation

This game can be verbal as a variation with each person taking their turn. Make it harder for the person after you with words like "box."

Rules:

Words in the train must be correctly spelled out—the referee is to arbitrate on any disputed spellings. Incorrect spellings cause that word and any others following it to be deducted from the total for that round. The longest train is that with the most "wagons" (words), not the most letters!

Average Speed Game

| 1+ | 11-99 | Hard |

The **Average Speed Game** is designed to keep older children occupied—as well as helping them with their schoolwork (but don't tell them that!). Adults can play along too.

Game play:

This game is played by calculating distances and trip times covered by a vehicle traveling at a given **average** speed. It is also possible to calculate the average speed of the car over a particular distance, if it is known how long the trip took (excluding any rest stops). Solve the problems on the opposite page. Using the simple formulae:

1) Speed x Time = Distance

2) Average Speed = $\dfrac{\text{Distance}}{\text{Time}}$ (Distance ÷ Time)

3) Time = $\dfrac{\text{Distance}}{\text{Speed}}$ (Distance ÷ Speed)

it is possible to figure out the time taken to cover a particular distance—if one is given the distance that is to be traveled and the average speed to be maintained. For example, a distance of 100 miles at an average speed of 40 mph will take 2.5 hours (100 miles ÷ 40 mph = 2.5 hours).

By using one of the other formulas, it is possible to calculate the average speed after having covered a known distance within a specified time. Similarly, the distance to be traveled at a known average speed, and within a given time period, can also be found.

Questions:

1) Jane drives at an average speed of 45 mph on a trip of 135 miles. How long does the trip take?

2) Chris rides his bicycle at an average speed of 8 mph. If he cycles for 6.5 hours, how far does he travel?

3a) Nikki has to travel a total of 351 miles. She travels the first 216 miles in 4 hours. What is her average speed for the first part of the trip?

3b) If her average speed is the same for the whole trip, how long does the whole trip take?

4) Jim travels 45 miles at 15 mph. How long does it take him?

5) Pamela walks at 4 mph for 2.5 hours. How far does she walk?

6) A car travels 300 miles in 5 hours. What is its average speed?

7) Calculate the distance traveled if you drove for 1.5 hours at 42 mph.

8) How long does it take to travel 385 miles at 70 mph?

(Answers are at the back of the book on page 154.)

Rules:

No calculators, laptops, or any other devices allowed—figure out the results using only your brainpower (or pencil and paper).

I Went to the Store

| 2+ | 4-99 | Medium |

I Went to the Store is also known as The Shopping Game. This is a game for all ages and can be played by players simply using the alphabet, their imagination, and their voices. A good memory is a distinct advantage!

Game play:

Before the game begins, the shopping items to be "bought" must first be chosen. In the examples shown below, the subject is "Food," although any item range that can be bought from a store can be used.

The game begins with the first player choosing a "food" item beginning with the letter "A." The player then says a line beginning with the words "I went to the store and I bought ... an Apricot."

The next player has to repeat the line "I went to the store and I bought an Apricot" and add to it a food item beginning with the letter "B," such as:

"I went to the store and I bought an Apricot ... and some Beans." The person whose turn is next has to repeat the line spoken by the previous player, then add a food item beginning with the letter "C," and so on.

Play continues until all of the letters of the alphabet have been used—or everybody has been stumped for ideas!

A whole range of subjects could be used. Just make sure that a reasonable sequence of alphabet letters is available for the first letters of the chosen subject, e.g. animals, with the leading phrase changed to suit the subject "I went to the zoo and I saw an Aardvark ... etc."

Variation

Singular and plural article to be used **alternately** for each new object, as in "... an Apricot ... some Beans ... a Cauliflower ..." etc., or, as a test of memory, a number could be used in sequence with the new letter of the alphabet.

"I went to the store and I bought 1 Apple" with the next player adding to the number and letter sequence: "I went to the store and I bought 1 Apple ... and 2 Bread rolls ... " and so forth.

Rules:

All players have to correctly say the complete list of items. Any player who gets an item wrong is out of the game. The winner is the last person who can repeat the list correctly and then add a new correct item of their own.

Highway Sign Mayhem

1+   7-99   Medium

Highway Sign Mayhem is a words and numbers game that can help to pass the time for adults and children who have the ability to make up different words from the letters that appear on signs, highway traffic signs, or billboards.

Game play:

Players have to make up a different word, or number of words, from those appearing on highway signs, traffic information signs on highways or main routes, or on billboards. A good starting point is to choose the first sign that appears after the next bridge or junction.

When the first sign or billboard is spotted, the players have to first write down the words on the sign. If there are too many words, choose just one line of words for the game. Players then have to make as many new words as they can from the chosen words on the sign or board. The letters may only be used the same number of times that they appear in the chosen word or phrase. A typical sign would be one that says "ROADWORK AHEAD." From these three words, players must write down as many words as they can make. A good tip is to write down the words in a word circle, as used by some people when trying to solve cryptic clues in word puzzle games.

In the example ROADWORK AHEAD the words DRAW, READ, HOOK are just three examples of words that can be made—try making some longer words for yourself!

Variation

Players to take turns at "translating" a sign in their own words, but keeping the same meaning by substituting each word with another. There is no need to write anything down—spontaneous translations are more fun! In the previous example, ROADWORK AHEAD could be changed to HIGHWAY MAINTENANCE IMMINENT.

R O A
D D
D W
A O
A R
E K
E H A K

Rules:

Remember, letters may only be used the same number of times that they appear in the chosen word or phrase.

Rhyming Words

1+   7-99   Medium

Rhyming Words can be played by any number of players. It is also a fun way of checking on their understanding of word sounds and associated letters recognition (particularly of those younger members of the group) without them really knowing!

Game play:

The game consists of players having to say words that look and/or sound the same as a given starting word. See if they can make words that rhyme with: HAIR (pair, chair, stair, etc.).

The player who makes the most rhyming words from the starting word is the winner of the first round and gets to choose the next word.

Rhyming words can be played as a team game or by individual players. The total number of rhyming words made, when added together, denotes the overall winner or team.

Rules:

Remember, the object of the game is to find words that rhyme: this includes words that are not necessarily formed with the same letter groups as the starting word. In the example given above (HAIR), the word "pear" rhymes with "hair" but has different letters. If the word sounds the same (rhymes.) it is allowed—but players have to spell out correctly to score a point. The same rule applies for alternative games played in which a starting letter is given.

Some examples of rhyming words are given here to get you started—but don't let the players see them—just give them the starting letters or word in **bold** print:

ub – cub, club, rub, scrub, shrub, stub, sub, tub

ar – are, afar, bar, car, far, guitar, jar, scar, star, tar

at – bat, combat, fat, flat, mat, pat, rat, sat, splat, that

in – begin, bin, chin, grin, pin, skin, thin, tin, twin, within

en – again, den, glen, hen, men, pen, ten, then, when, wren

all – all, ball, baseball, call, crawl, fall, hall, tall, small

an – an, began, can, fan, man, pan, plan, ran, scan, span, tan, van

et – bet, get, jet, let, met, pet, reset, set, threat, upset, wet, yet

ell – bell, farewell, fell, hotel, motel, sell, shell, smell, spell, well, yell

oze – bows, blows, flows, froze, grows, hose, nose, rose, those, toes

ap – cap, chap, clap, flap, gap, map, nap, slap, snap, strap, tap, trap, wrap, zap

it – admit, commit, bit, fit, flit, hit, it, kit, knit, lit, permit, pit, quit, sit, skit, slit, spit, split

and – band, bland, command, demand, expand, hand, land, sand, stand, understand

un – begun, bun, done, fun, gun, none, one, outdone, run, son, sun, ton, undone, won

ed – bed, bread, dead, fed, fled, head, instead, led, read, red, said, spread, thread, tread

ing – bring, cling, fling, king, ring, sing, sling, spring, sting, string, swing, thing, wing, zing

ite – bite, bright, delight, fight, fright, kite, knight, might, night, right, tight, tonight, white, write

ail – bale, detail, email, fail, hail, mail, male, nail, pail, rail, sail, scale, snail, stale, tale, whale

ot – bought, dot, forgot, fought, got, hot, knot, lot, not, pot, rot, taught, tot, shot, spot, squat

ound – around, crowned, found, ground, hound, mound, pound, round, sound, surround, wound

ate – ate, crate, create, date, fate, gate, great, late, mate, plate, rate, skate, slate, state, straight, trait, wait, weight

ack – attack, back, black, knack, lack, pack, quack, rack, sack, slack, smack, snack, stack, tack, track, whack, yak

air – aware, bare, beware, care, chair, compare, dare, declare, despair, fair, flare, hair, pair, prepare, rare, repair, scare, share, spare, square, stare, there, unfair, wear, where

Out for the Count

| | 2+ | 5-99 | Medium |

Out for the Count is a numbers game that also reinforces children's schoolwork and develops their ability for remembering number sequences.

Game play:

Each player is asked in turn to say the sequence of numbers that are between any two separated numbers. For younger players, these sequences should be fairly simple, say those from 1 to 10. To test their understanding, ask them to begin with a number from within that range, say from 3 to 8 or similar. A player who gets their sequence wrong has to try again!

Older players can be given more difficult sequences. For example, "backward" counting, odd and even, counting in fives—but starting on anything except a five, etc. The players can decide for themselves who is the winner!

Rules:

No writing down of numbers allowed! Fingers may be used if that helps!

Spelling Bee

2+	5-99	Medium	

Spelling Bee is a traditional favorite for all the family to play.

The first recorded **official** spelling bee occurred in 1925 when an 11-year-old boy named Frank Neuhauser won the 1st National Spelling Bee competition held in Washington DC. The nine finalists were invited to meet President Calvin Coolidge at the White House. This tradition has been followed by most of the presidents since that year.

Game play:

This game should be refereed by a parent or an older child with good word skills. Children then take turns at trying to spell a word that is suitable for their age group. It's more fun if tricky words are used for older players.

The game can be played between individual players or as a team game, but wherever possible, try to make sure that the teams are made up of players with similar spelling abilities.

Rules:

To avoid any arguments, the words could be taken from a book or newspaper and then shown to anybody who has a difference of opinion regarding its correct spelling. This could also be used to show the context in which that particular word is used.

SPEAKING AND IMAGINATION GAMES

One Line Each

Name Your Favorite

ABC of Places

Good News—Bad News

Guess What I Can See

20 Questions

Yes, Not No

Fast Alphabet

Name the Celebrity

Limericks and Poems

Who is it?

Silence is Golden

Yes! No! Game

Fantasy Fairy Tales

Find a Connection

One Line Each

2+   3-99   Easy

One Line Each is a simple speaking game that requires nothing other than an active imagination.

Game play:

One player starts the game with the first line of a story. The next player has to add a line of their own, and so on. It is better if the story is made up from the imaginations of the players, rather than trying to weave together some lines from known tales or stories. An example to start a game could be:

"Once upon a time there was a handsome Prince who was looking for a wife ..."

The next player could stay on the fairy-tale theme:

"He came to our house and asked if (girl's name) was in ..."

or they could change the story line to:

"He looked in the cupboard but all he found was ..."

The game can cover a variety of subjects, from nursery rhymes to fantasy tales about people you know—perhaps somebody in the car? They could relate to things seen on the trip, or things the children are going to do when they get to their destination.

Rules:

There are none—just make it all up as you go along!

Name Your Favorite

| 2+ | 3-99 | Easy |

Name Your Favorite is a game for players of all ages in which each person has to say who or what is their favorite person or thing—and then explain why!

Game play:

Before the game starts, it must be decided which category of "favorite" is to be the subject of the first round. Each player takes turns at telling the others who or what is their favorite in that category. When every player has had their turn, the group has to decide who gave the best reason for choosing that particular favorite.

Favorites can range from food or colors to cars, people, music, etc. The reasons given by a player for choosing their favorite in a category can be very informative, and will often be quite amusing to the others in the group, especially when the younger ones have their turn!

Rules:

Almost anything goes; just have fun. In the event of a disputed or tie vote on the best explanation, the referee has the final say!

ABC of Places

| 2+ | 5-99 | Medium |

ABC of Places is an interesting and absorbing game that requires players to name sequences of places around the world in alphabetical order of the first letter in the place name.

Game play:

The first player begins by listing as many different places as they can that begin with the letter "A" until they run out of ideas. No repeat names are allowed—if a player says the same place more than once, their turn ends, and the next player takes over. That player carries on until they also run out of names or mention a repeat name. As an example, for the letter "M," a series of names such as MICHIGAN, MOZAMBIQUE, MEXICO, MANCHESTER, and so forth is good. If a player repeats any of the names, such as MEXICO, their turn ends and the next player takes over. The new player may use any or all of the previous player's ideas!

When all players have had a turn with the letter "A," the person with the greatest number of "A" names starts off a new round of place names beginning with the letter "B." The game continues until all of the letters of the alphabet, or the players, are exhausted!

Variation

Each player, in turn, has to name a different place in the world beginning with each successive letter of the alphabet, until they either complete the alphabet or run out of ideas. The places can be a random selection of countries, cities, states, counties, or any other geographical features—this could include mountains, rivers, or similar. For instance, a random place list could include Australia, Birmingham, China, Detroit, Everest (mountain), Florida, and so forth.

Rules:

This is a knowledge-based memory game, so no books, atlases, or Internet devices allowed! Don't even think of inventing a place name either. In case of a dispute over the claimed name of a city or other geographical feature, that player has to state the name of the country in which that city or place can be found. A winner of a category or game gets to choose the next game to be played.

Good News— Bad News

2+   5-99   Medium

Good News—Bad News is a game in which players have to speak a line of a news broadcast—but with a twist!

Game play:

Decide who is going to start the game. The first player has to speak a line of "good news" and the next player has to follow on with a line of "bad news." For example:

"Here is the news for today—there will be free ice cream at the beach."—(Good news! ☺)

"But the bad news is—we are going to the mountains."—(Bad news ☹)

Using their imaginations, the following players have to keep giving alternating "good news" and "bad news" lines until everybody decides that the game is over. A new game can be started by a different player on a different topic—but remember not to let the same person give out the "good news" every time.

Rules:

Repeating a line or subject that has already been spoken is not allowed.

Guess What I Can See

2+   3-99   Easy

Guess What I Can See is a game in which players have to guess which object has been chosen by another person in the car. Clues are given as to the whereabouts or identity of the possible object as the car passes it.

Game play:

A simple game to play for all the family. A player must be chosen to begin the game—perhaps the winner of a previous game? This player must then silently choose an object as the car passes it. The object can be an animal in a field, a sign, another vehicle, or any thing. The object should not be a rarely seen item, because this could take too long to find and ruin the game for everybody.

As the car passes the object, the player who chose it has to give the clue by saying something like "There's one," or a similar phrase of the player's choosing. The guessers have to try to pick out what the object is from all the things that were visible as the car went past the point where the clue was given.

Because this is a test of observation and memory, it is better to wait until the object is about to be passed, rather than choosing something that is some distance ahead. A correct guess wins the round and the winner gets to choose the next object.

Rules:

The chooser must be honest and not change the object during the game. Items that are only in view for less than five seconds are not allowed.

20 Questions

2+	7-99	Medium

20 Questions is a classic, spoken quiz game that proved very popular as a radio program when it was first broadcast in the late 1940s. It can help improve the logical thought process in young and old alike.

Game play:

Before the game begins, one person is chosen to answer up to 20 questions posed by the remaining players. Each taking turns, the "questioners" seek to find the secret "identity" chosen by the "answerer." This secret identity can be that of a person, place, or thing, chosen by the answerer, in secret, before the questioning starts. It is helpful if the secret identity is written down before the inquisition begins, because this would make the game more transparent for all in the case of a dispute. The answerer can only reply "Yes" or "No" to each question.

If the questioners fail to find the secret identity after 20 questions have been answered, then the winner is the person who chose that secret identity: the answerer. If a player correctly guesses the identity by asking the winning question, then that person gets to choose the next secret identity.

Typical questions asked in this game are: 1) "Are you a person?" Answer: "No." 2) "Are you a manufactured article?" Answer: "No." Continue until 20 questions have been asked.

Cleverly worded questions can narrow down the possible, or the impossible, if properly thought through. Where younger children do not have the ability to ask a searching question that can only have a "Yes" or "No" answer, then the players can allow an answer of "Perhaps" or "Maybe" to give a better chance at a correct guess.

Variation

A popular variant of the game is **Animal, Vegetable, Mineral?** In this version, before the 20 questions begin, the answerer tells the questioners that the secret identity belongs to one or more of the animal, vegetable, or mineral kingdoms. An example of a "vegetable" object identity could be a table, because it is made from a naturally grown object: a tree. An object's identity can be both "animal" and "mineral" if the secret identity is a belt—this is made from leather (**animal**) and a buckle (metal, derived from a **mineral** source—iron ore).

Both games can be made as easy, or as difficult, as is necessary to take into account the ages of the players. Keep that in mind when selecting the secret identity or the animal, vegetable, or mineral objects.

Rules:

No peeking when the answerer writes down the secret identity! Always tell the truth, otherwise you will have to miss a turn at being the answerer in another game.

Yes, Not No

| 2+ | 5-99 | Easy |

Yes, Not No is a really fun game for the whole family.

Game play:

A player is chosen to be the "answerer." Each of the other players take turns at asking a leading question to which the answer would normally be "No"—but the answerer has to reply with the opposite meaning "Yes." Some creative imagination is needed to get the answerer to give the right (but wrong!) answer. A simple example would be a question asking: "Are you a mean person?"—to which the answer should be "No"—but in this game, the correct answer is "Yes."

Each player should try to think of a question that would evoke a silly answer. If the answerer gives the **wrong** answer (actually the "right" answer), then that player loses, and the player who asked that particular question becomes the next to answer the questions—see how long they can keep saying "Yes" when they really mean "No!"

Rules:

Try not to ask questions that could have two or more possibly conflicting answers. Keep it simple—it's more fun that way.

Fast Alphabet

2+	4-99	Easy

Fast Alphabet is a fast-talking game that can also be fun as the children can show off their command of the alphabet to everybody else in the car.

Game play:

Each player has to take turns at reciting the letters of the alphabet in as short a period of time as possible, without making a mistake. It is best played against the clock. The first player has to say all the letters of the alphabet as fast as they can, without making a mistake. As they get to the last letter (Z), the timekeeper announces the time taken. If the player makes a mistake, the other players make a "Buzz" noise; that player is out until the following round and the next person has their turn. Fastest alphabet wins the game.

Rules:

Before starting the game, a judge should be appointed to make sure that each alphabet is correctly recited—especially in the reverse alphabet variation.

Variation

For the more experienced or older players, recite the alphabet backward against the clock.

Name the Celebrity

2+   7-99   Medium

Name the Celebrity is a speaking game where each player has to follow on with the name of a celebrity that begins with the same initial as the last letter of the previous celebrity's name.

Game play:

Before the game begins, it should be agreed on which category of celebrity is to be named, or whether any random famous name is allowed.

The first player says the name of a famous person, for example, Brad Pitt. The next player has to say the name of another personality whose name begins with the last letter of the previous celebrity's name. In this case, the letter "t" from the last name "Pitt." So the next famous person could be President Thomas Jefferson, to be followed by a celebrity whose first name begins with the letter N, etc. So the celebrity name sequence could follow this pattern:

Brad Pitt—Thomas Jefferson—Neil Armstrong—Gwyneth Paltrow—W ...?

Any player who fails to follow with a correct leading initial for their celebrity or famous person (or who can not follow with a name at all!) is out of the game. If a player follows on with a name that has the same initial letter for both their first name and last name such as Donald Duck, then this reverses the order of play. A player giving a third consecutive double answer is out!

The player who is the last person standing at the end of the game is the winner and gets to choose a celebrity category for the next round.

Variation

Variations on this game are almost endless. The chosen category of celebrity name could be almost anything: from those living or dead, characters from history, classic novels, movie stars, politicians, singers or musicians, cartoon characters, or any other group that comes to mind. Game play is the same for all categories—unless the players can think of a different way of playing the game!

Rules:

Celebrities must be well known to all players, particularly when there are younger players in the game. If challenged, the player declaring the celebrity name has to explain which field of the arts, profession, or history their person became famous in.

Limericks and Poems

2+   **5-99**   Medium

Limericks and Poems can provide a great deal of creative fun for all the family. It is useful for improving the language skills of younger children, but can be played and enjoyed by young and old alike.

Limericks are said to have originated in the town of Limerick in Ireland, and were originally bar songs, sung by those who had drunk too much. This gave the limerick a well-deserved bad reputation that was somewhat legitimized by the likes of William Shakespeare, who used them in his plays **Othello** and **King Lear**, and Edward Lear, who wrote a famous volume of limericks in 1846.

Game play:

Limericks are short poems that traditionally have only five lines of verse. Lines 1, 2, and 5 of Limericks have 7-10 syllables and rhyme with one another. Lines 3 and 4 of Limericks have 5-7 syllables and also rhyme with each other. Players have to each make up their own limerick using the guidelines above. An example would be as follows:

There was a Young Lady whose chin,
Resembled the point of a pin;
So she had it made sharp,
And purchased a harp,
And played several tunes with her chin.

– Edward Lear

74

The best limerick wins the round.

If the limericks have stimulated the imaginations of the children in the car, try getting them to each make up a poem of their own using a given theme, such as the weather, animals, the trip itself, or any other subject. That should keep them amused for a while! When they have completed their poems, get them to take turns at reciting their poem aloud for the benefit of all. Best poem wins.

> Come to me, O ye children!
> For I hear you at your play,
> And the questions that perplexed me
> Have vanished quite away.
>
> – Henry Wadsworth Longfellow

Who is it?

| 2+ | 5-99 | Easy |

Who is it? is a guessing game in which the players have to guess the identity of a person by asking questions to which the answers can only be "Yes" or "No."

Game play:

One player is picked to start the game. This person chooses the name of a person whose name is known to the other players. These players then take turns at asking a question in an attempt to find out who that mystery person could be. The answer to their questions can only be either "Yes" or "No."

For example, if the chosen mystery person is a friend, the questioners have to first establish whether the group knows the person: "Do I know you?"—the answer is "Yes." "Are you a boy?"—the answer is "No"—this indicates that the person is a girl who is known to the questioners. The game can be played using the identities of friends, family, famous celebrities, in fact anybody—alive or dead. If the identity is discovered, then the player who guessed it correctly chooses the next mysterious person.

Rules:

Only "Yes" or "No" answers are allowed. Players must ask their questions with this rule in mind—compound questions such as "Are you alive or dead?" cannot be answered with the words "Yes" or "No!"

Silence is Golden

2+   3-99   Hard

Silence is Golden is the favorite game of parents and anyone who spends long car rides with children. On a long trip it can give a little respite to the harassed grown-ups! They can play this game too.

Game play:

The game can be played by any number of players, whether children or adults. Before the game begins, it must be decided how long the game will last. A time limit or the distance to the next rest stop is a good idea—the prospect of a prize (otherwise known as bribery) at the end of the game should ensure that most (but probably not all) players make an effort to be the winner.

The game begins with a 5-4-3-2-1-0 countdown to silence—this lets all the players have one last chance to shout out, before the welcome and much needed silence starts. The last player to speak, or make a vocal noise, is the winner.

Rules:

No talking after the countdown ends—this includes giggling, whistling, humming, or any other vocal sound. Any player trying to cause another player to make a vocal noise, by unfair means, does not get a prize at the end of the trip. Enjoy the game!

Yes! No! Game

2+   5-99   Easy

Yes! No! is a fun game for all of the family. It is a question and answer game where the object is to answer questions without using either "Yes" or "No."

Game play:

One player is chosen to be the first answerer. The other players then take turns at asking the questions or, if preferred, one player can be the questioner. The questioner asks a series of questions in an attempt to trick the answerer into replying either "Yes" or "No," such as:

"What is your name?" (The answerer gives their name.)

"Are you sure?" (The answerer should not say "Yes," instead—something like "I am!")

"Are you certain?" (The answerer should not say "Yes" but instead give a confirmatory reply.)

The questioner continues with questions such as:

"Do you like hot dogs?" (Answerer replies without saying "Yes" or "No.")
"Do you like them with ketchup?" (Reply.)
"Are you sure?" (Reply) etc.

If the answerer uses either "Yes" or "No" to any question, the other players say "Buzz!" and that person loses their turn. The player with the longest sequence of replies without using the words "Yes" or "No" wins the game.

Rules:

Do not ask questions that require more than one answer. The answerer should not keep repeating the same reply, otherwise they lose the round by default. The answerer must reply within five seconds, otherwise they get the "Buzz" from the other players!

Fantasy Fairy Tales

2+   3-99   Medium

Fantasy Fairy Tales gives each player the opportunity to let their creative imagination run free as they invent their own fantasy story.

A fairy tale is a short story or tale based on characters from folklore, including fairies, elves, goblins, and trolls. There is always an element of magic or enchantment in this type of story.

Game play:

Each player takes turns at making up a fantasy fairy tale. The tale should be as imaginative or far-fetched as they can possibly make it. Players should bring into their tale some fantastic events or creative ideas that would not be found in real life. This includes dragons, witches and wizards, magic spells and potions, treasure chests, and enchanted castles—just let the imagination run wild—the more fantastic the better. At the end of the round, the other players decide who is the winner by voting for their favorite story.

Variation

Create a story as a team and make sure you make each person contribute, perhaps by doing two to three lines each.

Rules:

Each fantasy fairy tale must be thought up by the player telling the tale. Characters from other tales may be "borrowed"—but the tale itself must be the work of the individual player.

Find a Connection

2+   4-99   Medium

Find a Connection is a word game in which the players have to link a series of objects that have a logical connection to the previous word.

Game play:

A player is chosen to begin the game by nominating a word. The next player has to find other words that connect to it, in a sequence, without repeating a previously mentioned word and without undue hesitation.

As an example, if the chosen word is "Bird," the player has to find a word that connects to it, and then find another word that follows on in a "connection" with the previous word. A logical sequence following on from "Bird" could be:

Bird Crow Nest Eggs Omelet ...

In the sequence given, each word has some connection with the word immediately preceding it: a **crow** is a type of bird, a crow builds a **nest** in which **eggs** are laid, and an **omelet** is made from eggs, and so forth.

If a player hesitates, or repeats a previous word in the connection sequence, then they lose, and is out of that round. Hesitation is a period longer than a count of three—or any number agreed before the game, always keeping in mind that younger players may need a little bit longer to think of a connection.

Variation

Players each think of as many objects as they can that are linked (or connected) to the same initial letter. The first player starts with a letter that is chosen before the game, for example the letter "F." They then have to name as many objects as they can that begin with "F": Field, Folder, Fly, Fence, etc. The player scores a point for each object name they can say above a total of six words (or any number agreed before the game), until they run out of ideas. That player then chooses the letter for the next player's turn. If a player fails to name at least six (or an agreed number) of objects, the game passes to the next player, who can then use the same objects as they attempt to reach the target number of items, from the same initial letter of the alphabet.

Rules:

No dictionaries or electronic devices are allowed. Younger children are allowed to use phonics!

ACTION GAMES AND ACTIVITIES

Hands, Faces, and Fingers Games:

86–101

Singing Games:

102–117

Hands, Faces, and Fingers Games

Rock, Paper, Scissors

Simon Says

Don't Say a Word

Do What I Do

Waving Game

1—2—3—Shoot

Funny Faces

Straight Face

Charades

Fortune-Teller

Rock, Paper, Scissors

	2+	4-99	Easy

Rock, Paper, Scissors, is a well-known hand game, played by two or more people, and is often used as a method of selection instead of tossing a coin.

The game is believed to have been played in the Han dynasty in China in the 2nd century BC according to a book written during the Ming dynasty between the 14th and the 17th century AD. Originally known as "The Gestures," it was played almost universally by the middle of the 20th century. In some countries, a different series of objects, but always in an "odd" number combination (usually of three or sometimes five) are used. Whatever the number, the game is essentially the same.

Game play:

Each player makes a fist with one hand. On a count of three, the players raise their fisted hand and swing it downward on each number of the count. After the count of "Three," somebody says the trigger word "Shoot!" (or another word of the players' choosing), whereupon the players change their hands, instantly and simultaneously, into one of the three gestures that represent either Rock, Paper, or Scissors, and throw it in the direction of their opponent(s).

The gestures are:

- Rock, represented by a clenched fist gesture.
- Paper, represented by a horizontally held open hand, with the four fingers straightened and touching each other.
- Scissors, represented by two fingers extended from the fist and separated.

The object of the game is to choose a gesture that defeats that of an opponent. The hierarchy of the gestures is as follows:

- Rock breaks scissors, therefore, rock defeats scissors.
- Paper can wrap around a rock, therefore, paper defeats rock.
- Scissors cut paper, so scissors defeats paper.

Best of three, or five rounds, wins the game.

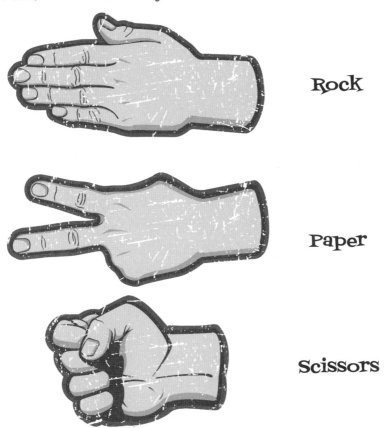

Rock

Paper

Scissors

Rules:

If both players choose the same gesture, then the result is a tie, and the next round takes place. No hanging back to see the opponent's gesture is allowed—players must make their gestures simultaneously. By clever anticipation, it may be possible to "read" a player's mind, and beat them that way!

Simon Says

3+   3-99   Easy

Simon Says is a game for three or more players. One of the players assumes the role of "Simon" and the other players follow Simon's instructions to perform certain actions—but only if preceded by the trigger phrase "Simon says ... " A psychological study has found that the game can be a healthy way to help children to improve their self-control and restrain their impulsive behavior.

The game was first played in Roman times when the Latin phrase "Cicero dicit fac hoc" ("Cicero says do this") was used—Cicero being a powerful political figure who issued decrees. More recent times saw the first use of the name Simon: this dates back to the year 1264, when Simon de Montfort captured the English king Henry III, and held him in Lewes Castle in Sussex, England. Until retaken by Henry's son Prince Edward, the usurper Simon de Montfort was able to issue commands and decrees as if King Henry himself made them—hence the term "Simon says."

Game play:

One player is chosen to play "Simon"—perhaps the winner of the previous game. This player gives the action commands, preceded by the trigger phrase "Simon says ...," as in "Simon says, lift up your arms" and the other players have to do as Simon says! The player who is Simon has to try to trick the other players into performing a movement without him or her having first said "Simon says," as in "Stick out your tongue."

If Simon says only the command words, without first saying the trigger phrase, then any player who either moves or carries out that command is out of the game. The last player left in the game is the winner—although it is possible that **both** of the last two players left in the game will either move or carry out the commanded movement. In this case, the person playing Simon plays the next round of the game in that role.

Rules:

Because this game is being played in the car, players who are "Simon" should not ask the others to do anything that is dangerous to either themselves or any another player, or do anything that would distract the driver.

Don't Say a Word

| 3+ | 5-99 | Medium |

Don't Say a Word is a miming game in which players have to tell a story or answer questions without using a particular word.

Game play:

Write the chosen "silent" word on a piece of paper. Each player takes turns at nominating the subject of a story that must be told by each player in turn, without using the silent word. When they get to the part of the story that contains the silent word, the player has to act out in mime what the word represents. This mime can be played out using hand movements or facial expressions but no words are to be used during the mime part of the story. All of the players in each round have to tell their own version of the story, using a different mime, in place of the silent word.

Any subject can be chosen for the story being told, but choose the silent word carefully to see how the players interpret it in mime. It should be a word that is likely to occur more than once in the story. One of the simplest words to mime is the personal pronoun "I." Make things a little more difficult by choosing a common, such as "saw" and then choose a story subject, such as "I went to the movies." The word "saw" can be mimed in several different ways, by miming a sawing action, or by pointing to the eyes first, then toward another object.

Several variations can be played, still using miming gestures. These can include the players each having to mime a complete line from a short story, such as "I went to the theater, and saw a movie." If the car happens to be passing a movie theater that would be really lucky. The next player then has to mime something on the lines of "The movie was the **Three Musketeers**," and so forth.

Apart from facial expressions, the players can use their fingers to show numbers, or to point at a clue during their mime. The game is only for fun, but players can vote for whoever delivers the most original mime.

Variation
Ask each player to mime a particular word or expression. This will help younger players get used to the idea of the game.

Rules:
Strictly no speaking during the mime—don't say a word!

Do What I Do

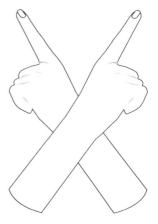

2+   4-99   Easy

Do What I Do is a copycat actions game that keeps the children occupied and provides a few minutes of precious respite for the driver.

Game play:

One player is chosen to start the game. This player has to make a particular series of gestures using their hands, fingers, head movements, and facial gestures. Each of the other players then has to repeat the actions performed by the first player. The person who led off then decides which player has best copied their actions. The winner is the person who correctly follows the first person's gestures or actions and that player starts the next round.

The gestures should follow a particular sequence, as in: two nods of the head, followed by first raising one hand and arm to the front, then two more nods of the head, etc. It is surprising how imaginative children can be while playing this game. If young children are playing the game, try to keep the sequence of actions fairly short.

Rules:

No touching another player; be especially careful when moving the arms around. Prompting is not allowed either (except to encourage the little ones!).

Waving Game

2+   2-99   Easy

Waving Game is a game that children will love to play. The game requires no particular skill, but needs a lot of enthusiasm from the players. It is quite rewarding when the people in the other cars wave back!

Game play:

The game can be played just for fun or as a competition. In the fun game, every player has to wave at the people in passing cars. If they wave back, everybody in the car cheers and then waves back at them. This game is particularly good whenever your car is stopped at a traffic light—especially when a bus with a lot of passengers passes by!

The game can also be played when only the front-seat passenger does the waving. Individual players or teams can then nominate an oncoming vehicle with more than one person onboard to be waved at by the front-seat passenger in your car. If anybody in the other vehicle waves back, the player or team that picked the car to be waved at scores a point. In a team game, the players in both teams should each take turns at nominating the vehicle to be waved at—this avoids any confusion.

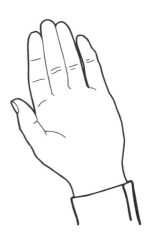

Rules:
Drivers should not play this game. No horn blowing or flashing of lights to attract the attention of people in other cars is allowed. Leave at least one vehicle between turns—this will ensure that the game is fair for all.

1—2—3—Shoot

3+   4-99   Easy

1—2—3—Shoot is believed to have originated in bars, when it was used to decide whose turn it was to buy the next round of drinks.

Game play:

While there are many variations of 1—2—3—Shoot, most forms can be played with two, three, or more players. The most common version involves all players at a given command, usually "1—2—3—Shoot!," throwing out a single hand showing either zero or a number of fingers. The first person to guess the correct total of fingers displayed wins one point. The first player to win three points is the winner of the game.

Variation

A popular variation for two players is called "Odds and Evens," where one player is designated the "odds" player and the other is the "evens" player. On the command "1—2—3—Shoot," both players hold out either one or two fingers. If the total number of fingers is an odd number, the "odds" player wins the round—otherwise the "evens" player is the winner.

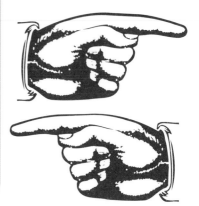

Rules:

Only the fingers of one hand can be used.

Funny Faces

2+ 2-99 Easy

Funny Faces is a game in which each player tries to make the funniest face—usually won by grandpa or the youngest player!

Game play:

A simple game to play. Each player in the car has to take turns at making a face that is funny or silly to look at. After the first round, the players have to decide who pulled the funniest face. The winner starts off the next round of the game.

Variation

Players in the car can decide who has the funniest face in a passing car or waiting at a bus stop, but beware!—they may be playing the same game and could be choosing a funny face from your car!

Rules:

No props or artificial aids to funniness allowed.

A cheetah.

Straight Face

2+   2-99   Easy

Straight Face involves the whole group. The object of the game is to try to make someone laugh. Easy? Just try it!

Game play:

One player must be chosen to start the game. He or she has to try to make a straight face—then keep it straight, while the other players attempt to make the "straight face" player laugh or smile (or perhaps frown). The person who succeeds in making the first player laugh, smile, or otherwise change their facial expression is the winner and takes the next turn to be Straight Face.

Try getting them to smile or laugh by asking them strange and silly questions—or even noises?

Variation

All of the players play at the same time. The player who keeps their straight face the longest wins.

Rules:

Other players can do almost anything to make a "straight face" break their expression. They can themselves make funny faces, say something funny, or whatever. Touching the person who is "straight face" is not allowed—so no tickling!

Charades

2+   5-99   Medium

Charades needs little or no explanation, as most children are aware of the art of charades.

Game play:

First, each player has to secretly write down a topic on a small piece of paper. These topics are then mixed into a random pile without the players being able to see the written words. The first player then has to select a piece of paper and, still keeping it hidden from the other players, has to act out the topic that is written on their piece of paper. The first person to guess the topic gets to take the next turn. Each player has to mime a topic—if none of the other players guesses a player's topic, that mime artist loses and has to sit out the remainder of the round.

Rules:

No peeking while your nearest (or any other!) player is writing down their topic. If a player pulls out the piece of paper with their own topic, that is the luck of the game.

Fortune-Teller

1+   5-99   Medium

Fortune-Teller is an entertaining game that tests both the concentration skills and the imagination of the players, as they make their own "fortune-teller" from a sheet of plain paper using a form of origami.

Game play:

First of all, each player has to make their own fortune-teller by following the instructions below and the diagram.

The corners of a sheet of paper (1) are folded up to meet the opposite sides (2 & 3) and (if the paper is not already square) the top is cut or carefully torn off (4), making a square sheet with diagonal creases (5).

The four corners of the paper are folded into the middle of the square (6), being careful not to go beyond the crease lines. This forms a shape known in origami as a blintz base or cushion fold (7). The resulting smaller square is turned over (8), and the four corners are folded in toward the center a second time (9) & (10). All four corners are folded up so that the points meet in the middle (11), and the player works their fingers into the pockets of paper in each of the four corners (12). The finished fortune-teller shape is then ready to receive the decoration and numbers or colors to be written on the fortune-teller according to the player's own choices.

The inside eight triangles should either be numbered from one to eight, or given colors either by name, or by coloring in the flap. Underneath each of the flaps a prediction of the future for the person whose fortune is to be told should be written—this can be: you will be rich and famous or, you will meet a tall stranger, etc. Make sure that the writing fits inside the triangle immediately under the selected fortune number or color.

To use the fortune-teller, the player telling the fortunes holds the four corners of the origami fortune-teller by inserting their index finger and a thumb from each hand into the pockets on the underside (12). Keeping two pairs of corners together, the other two pairs are then separated so that only four of the numbered or colored triangles are visible. The fingers and thumbs are then opened and closed in opposing pairs, so that the numbers or colors that are visible alternate with each movement.

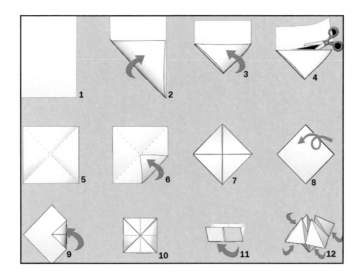

A person asks the question "Can you tell me my fortune?" of the person holding the fortune-teller. The holder of the fortune-teller then asks for a number or color. Once the number or color is chosen, the holder uses their fingers to switch between the two groups of colors and numbers inside the fortune-teller. The holder switches the position of the device the requested number of times. This is either the number chosen itself or the number of letters in the name of the color chosen.

Once the holder has finished switching the positions of the fortune-teller, the player chooses one of the flaps revealed. These flaps are those that have colors or numbers on them. The holder then lifts the flap and reveals the fortune underneath.

Singing Games

Three Blind Mice
Row Your Boat
The Wheels on the Bus
Old MacDonald
Hey Diddle Diddle
It's Raining, It's Pouring
iPod Intros
Sing a Song With ??? in the Title
Name that Tune
Spoken Lyrics

Three Blind Mice

1+   3-99   Easy

Three Blind Mice is a traditional nursery rhyme that has its origins in English history some time before the beginning of the 17th century.

Game play:

The song can be sung by children of almost all ages—actions are permitted, and even encouraged, during the song!

For those who haven't heard the song, the lyrics are given below. The song can be repeated several times so that each singer can be a soloist. For more than one singer, they can either sing one line each or all together—but don't forget the actions!

Variation

A more complicated version for older children is for them to sing the song as a "round," a type of song where each singer joins in, in turn, stating their first line when the previous singer is starting their second line, and so forth. Try it—it can be chaotic but is a lot of fun for all!

Three blind mice. Three blind mice.
See how they run. See how they run.
They all ran after the farmer's wife,
Who cut off their tails with a carving knife,
Did you ever see such a thing in your life,
As three blind mice?

Row Your Boat

	1+	3-99	Easy

Row Your Boat is a traditional nursery rhyme or folk song. Its full title is Row, Row, Row Your Boat and it is usually sung as a "round." Dating from the mid-19th century, the version best known today was first published in 1881.

Game play:

This song is often sung with children sitting on the floor and facing each other in pairs. Joining hands, they then rock backward and forward, as if in a rowing boat, as they sing the song. For car travel, it is recommended that the participants simply use their arms to act out the necessary rowing motion—perhaps this version could be played at a rest stop or picnic area? Repeat the song as many times as you like!

Row, row, row your boat,
Gently down the stream.
Merrily, merrily, merrily, merrily,
Life is but a dream.

The Wheels on the Bus

1+   3-99   Easy

The Wheels on the Bus is a popular song with children everywhere and is believed to have been based on the traditional British folk song **Here We Go Round the Mulberry Bush.**

Game play:

This game should be accompanied by gestures and sound effects to suit each verse of the song.

> The wheels on the bus go round and round,
> round and round,
> round and round.
> The wheels on the bus go round and round,
> all over town.
>
> The wipers on the bus go swish, swish, swish,
> swish, swish, swish,
> swish, swish, swish.
> The wipers on the bus go swish, swish, swish,
> all over town.
>
> The horn on the bus goes, beep, beep, beep ...
> The money on the bus goes, clink, clink, clink ...
> The driver on the bus says, "Tickets please" ...
> The babies on the bus say, "Wah, wah, wah" ...
> The mommies on the bus say, "Shush, shush, shush" ...

Old MacDonald

| | 1+ | 4-99 | Easy |

Old MacDonald is a children's song about a farmer named MacDonald and the animals he keeps on his farm. This song is a particular favorite with children because they add the animal noises along with the words of the song. The first recorded version appeared around 1917 in a collection of World War 1 songs written by F. T. Nettleingham, entitled Ohio, about a farmer from that state called MacDougal:

Old Macdougal had a farm in Ohio-i-o,
And on that farm he had some dogs in Ohio-i-o,
With a bow-wow here, and a bow-wow there,
Here a bow, there a wow, everywhere a bow-wow.

Game play:

The modern words of the song are:

Old MacDonald had a farm, EE-I-EE-I-O,
And on that farm he had a [animal name], EE-I-EE-I-O,
With a [animal noise twice] here and a [animal noise twice] there,
Here a [animal noise], there a [animal noise], everywhere a
[animal noise twice],
Old MacDonald had a farm, EE-I-EE-I-O.

If the animal is a cow:

Old MacDonald had a farm, EE-I-EE-I-O,
And on that farm he had a cow, EE-I-EE-I-O,
With a moo moo here and a moo moo there,
Here a moo, there a moo, everywhere a moo moo,
Old MacDonald had a farm, EE-I-EE-I-O.

And so on for each new animal (there are a lot of them!).

Hey Diddle Diddle

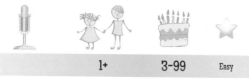

| 1+ | 3-99 | Easy |

Hey Diddle Diddle is another old English rhyme or folk song. The earliest recorded appearance of the poem was in **Mother Goose's Melody** in London in 1765, although two of its lines were referred to in a book dated 1569:

> "They be at hand Sir with stick and fidle;
> They can play a new dance called hey-didle-didle."

The modern version is:

> Hey diddle diddle,
> The cat and the fiddle,
> The cow jumped over the moon,
> The little dog laughed to see such a sport,
> And the dish ran away with the spoon.

While the original version was:

> High diddle diddle,
> The cat played the fiddle,
> The cow jump'd over the moon,
> The little dog laugh'd to see such craft,
> And the dish ran away with the spoon.

Sing either or both versions—small children love it, especially when they are told to think about the characters as they sing the song.

It's Raining, It's Pouring

| | 1+ | 4-99 | Easy |

It's Raining, It's Pouring originated in the late 1930s.

Game play:

There are two versions of this song—choose whichever is preferred by your youngest players.

> It's raining, it's pouring.
> The old man is snoring.
> He went to bed and bumped his head,
> And he couldn't get up in the morning.

Alternative version has line 3 altered as in:

> It's raining, it's pouring.
> The old man is snoring.
> He bumped his head and went to bed,
> And he couldn't get up in the morning.

iPod Intros

2+	7-99	Easy

iPod Intros is a relatively modern game that is particularly suited to older children—but the younger ones may be able to play along too! The game is a test of the players' overall knowledge of music of whatever genre they, or the adults, have on their personal music player, whether this is an iPod or any other type of MP3 player.

Game play:

One person is nominated to be in control of the music player. The music player should be set to "shuffle" or "random" play for the tracks, because this is the best way of finding out how well a player knows the world of music.

The first game is one in which the first player to identify the opening few notes of the introductory music to a track gains a point. The controller starts to play a track but lets only the first two or three notes sound before pressing the pause button. If nobody can identify the title **and** the artist, the controller plays a few more notes of the track, and so on, until a guesser correctly identifies both the title and artist of the track. The first player to get to 10 points (or whatever number is previously decided) is the winner.

Another method of game play is for each player, in turn, to try to sing the first line of the song as the intro leads into it—any wrong words (or out of tune singing) loses a point for the singer. First to score 10 points is the winner.

Variation

The iPod controller pauses the music track at random intervals during the track. The next player in turn has to sing the next line, or phrase, of the track—if it is an instrumental track, then the player has to hum the next few notes of the tune.

Rules:

Keep the volume at a reasonable level to avoid annoying the driver—this applies to the singing or humming **and** the music player volume.

Sing a Song With ??? in the Title

	2+	3-99	Hard

Sing a Song With ??? in the Title is a singing quiz-type game where the players have to perform a song with the chosen word ??? in it, as picked by the previous player.

Game play:

A player is chosen to name the first ??? word in a song title. The word they choose must be part of a recognized song title that should be familiar to the other players.

The ??? word can be chosen from a whole range of subjects. Examples of suitable words could be along the lines of colors: blue (as in Blue Moon), or objects. Just think of a difficult subject that you **know** has a song about it—but it must be mentioned in the **title** of that song, not simply in the lyrics.

When the first person has chosen the name within a title, that person says, "Sing a song with (the chosen word) in the title." The next player has to sing the first line or two of the song that has the chosen word in its title within, say, a five-second countdown. If the player fails to come up with a song, that player misses their turn. The next player tries to follow on with their song but **without** a countdown. This is because every player should have had sufficient time to think up their own song title.

If the chosen word happened to be "Rose," the song could be **Every Rose has its Thorn**—but do you know it? Perhaps **Bed of Roses** is familiar?

Variation

Pick more obscure words and find a song with that word anywhere within its lyrics.

Rules:

Plurals and singular words, in the song sung by a player, are allowed provided the plural is partly spelled out with the same order of letters as in the chosen word. Sound-alikes (as in pair or pear) are not allowed—the song must contain the chosen word in its title in its correct spelling, except for plurals as above.

Name that Tune

| | 2+ | 7-99 | Hard |

Name that Tune is based on a popular television game show. The TV version used an orchestra to play a nominated number of notes of a tune for the contestants to guess and had large cash prizes available to the winner. This version needs no orchestra—the players give the musical clues in a different form.

Game play:

In this version of the game, the orchestra is replaced by one of the players. That player then hums or whistles a number of notes from a popular tune. The number of notes to be performed is that number selected by the player whose turn it is. It is better to pick a fairly large number of notes at first to get the game started.

A player says to the performer, "I'll name that tune in **five**" (five notes), or any number of notes they choose. The performer then hums or whistles the first five notes of a tune. If the player guesses the tune correctly, he or she wins the round and becomes the performer for the next round. If they fail to identify the tune, the performer wins and gets to perform the next tune. Points can be awarded for a win, or deducted for a losing guess.

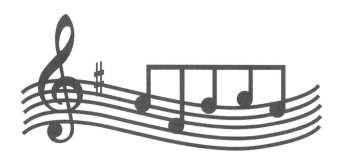

For games with two or more players, not including the performer, the players can bid against each other in a downward succession of guesses in an attempt to outsmart their opponents—but, if they fail to guess the tune, they lose as many points as there are opponents in the game. If they win by guessing the tune correctly, they gain a point for every opponent they have defeated.

Rules:
Time limit of one minute for each guess.

Spoken Lyrics

	2+	7-99	Hard

Spoken Lyrics is a music game with a difference. Instead of singing the words of a song, players have to speak them!

Game play:

Players decide who is first to take a turn at being the orator. This player then has to challenge the other players to identify a well-known song by speaking some of the lyrics. The words spoken should be in a dramatic or disguised manner, said in a way that breaks up the normal rhythm of the song. Even the words of very well-known songs can be disguised by simply changing the emphasis of key words. The first player to correctly identify the song wins the round and gets to perform the next oration.

Sample lyrics are given below as examples to start the game. Try speaking the lines without using the original song rhythm: use a Shakespearean actor's delivery or say it in a funny voice!

(Oops!)... I did it
again I played with your heart,
got lost
in the game Oh
baby,
baby (Oops!)
You think I'm in
love that I'm sent from
above I'm not
that (innocent)

(– from the Britney Spears song, **Oops!... I Did It Again**—Lyrics © Max Martin & Remi Yacoub)

Try omitting the giveaway words in brackets to make it really difficult! Even fairly well-known songs take on a different feel when treated in this manner. Have a try for yourself with these lines just to get the feel for changing the intonation of the lyrics. Those given here are in their original form—just simply rework the line structure, the punctuation, or the timing, then practice saying them in an unusual tone of voice:

When I want you in my arms
When I want you and all your charms
Whenever I want you
All I have to do is dream
Dream, dream, dream

(from **All I Have To Do Is Dream**—Lyrics © House of Bryant Publications

Now think of some for yourself—and good luck in the game!

Rules:

No obscure verses allowed, use only main verses or chorus words.

PUZZLES AND DRAWING GAMES

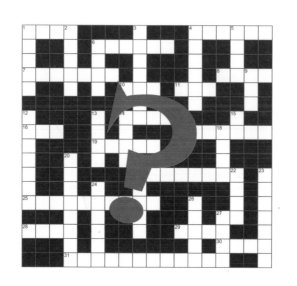

Tic Tac Toe

Close the Box

Hangman

Battleships

Pass Around the Drawing

Guess What I'm Drawing

Tic Tac Toe

| | 2 | 4-99 | Medium |

Tic Tac Toe is a simple, yet absorbing game for almost all ages—but its limited scope makes it more suitable for younger children as they begin to work out the game tactics for themselves. The game is believed to have originated in Roman times around the 1st century BC.

Game play:

A 3 x 3 grid is drawn on a piece of paper. Two players X and O take turns at marking their symbol in one of the spaces of the grid. The first player to place their symbol in a position that creates a straight line of three symbols wins the game. It is most satisfying when a player gets a winning line of three symbols and is then able to draw a line through their sequence of three symbols.

It is traditional for the player who is X to take the first turn, so this must be decided before the game starts. To avoid disputes, alternate the players between X and O if needed.

Rules:

Only one symbol from each player can be placed in any one turn. Only **straight** lines of three Xs or Os win the game.

In the following example X wins the game:

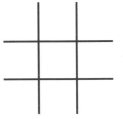

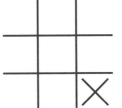

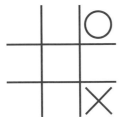

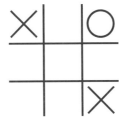

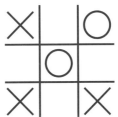

Close the Box

2+   6-99   Medium

Close the Box is a simple grid-style strategy drawing game. The game involves the players in working out tactics that result in their being able to close a square box by drawing straight lines between two adjacent points.

Game play:

One player draws a grid composed of dots on a sheet of paper. If squared or graph paper is available, use that. Grids can be of any size but choose wisely—the more dots, the longer the game! The page opposite could be photocopied before departing.

Each player then takes turns at drawing a straight line between any two adjacent dots, but only in a horizontal or vertical direction. The game becomes more interesting—and more difficult!—as more and more lines are drawn.

The object of the game is for a player to draw the last line that closes a box. When this occurs, the player who closes the box writes their initial inside that box to claim it as theirs. When all boxes have been closed, the game is over and the initials are counted to find who has closed the most boxes, and is, therefore, the winner.

As this is a strategy game, players should try to deceive their opponents into thinking that they are intending to close a particular box when, in fact, they are intending to close a box elsewhere on the grid.

Rules:

Only two adjacent dots or intersections on a grid may be joined by a line; larger squares are not allowed. Neither are diagonals! The object is to close boxes, not triangles—unless you can create your own game using that particular method!

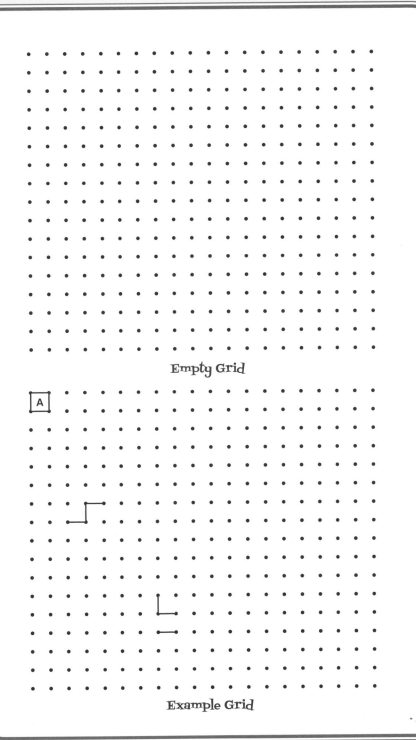

Empty Grid

A

Example Grid

Hangman

| 2 | 5-99 | Medium |

Hangman is a pencil and paper guessing game in which one player thinks of a word and the other player has to try to guess it by suggesting a series of letters that it may contain. The game is believed to have originated in Victorian times when it was sometimes called **Gallows**.

Game play:

Each player starts the game by drawing a gallows and rope shape as in (1) on the diagram. The first player chosen to start the game thinks of a word and tells the opponent how many letters it contains and then draws the same number of dashes under the gallows shape as there are letters in the word.

The guesser then chooses a letter thought to be in the word—a vowel is a good start. The word chooser then says whether that letter is in the word—if it is, he tells the guesser which position(s) that letter occupies in the word and then writes that letter or multiple instances of it above the dash that denotes its position within the word.

If the letter does not form part of the word, the chooser says "Wrong!" and has to draw the first part of the hangman (2)—in this case, the head. For each wrong guess, another body part must be added to the drawing (3) to (6). The game continues with the guesser choosing letters until either the word is correctly guessed or the hangman is completed (7). In the case of the hangman being completed, the guesser loses that game.

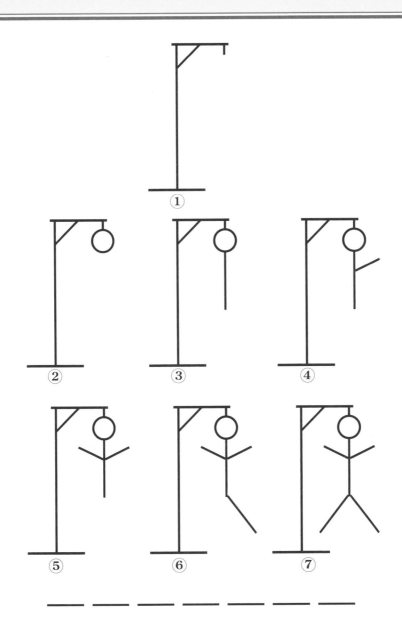

___   ___   ___   ___   ___   ___   ___

Rules:

The chooser must correctly declare the position of the letter guessed. If the letter occurs more than once in the word, this must also be declared, along with each position the letter appears in the word.

Battleships

2	5-99	Medium

Battleships, otherwise known as **Sea Battle**, is a guessing game for two people. It is a pencil and paper game that uses a player's intuition and strategic skills to sink an opponent's fleet of ships.

Game play:

The game is played on squared grids, usually of 10 x 10 squares each. Both players draw two grids each on their own sheet of paper exactly as shown in the diagram opposite with the letters and numbers along the sides and tops. The page opposite could be photocopied before departing.

Before the game begins, each player secretly marks his own grid (My Ships) with an agreed complement of ships. Traditionally, the ships occupy a number of squares according to their size—**Aircraft Carrier = 5 Squares; Battleship = 4; Cruiser = 3; Destroyer = 3; Submarine = 2**—or as agreed before the game begins. Usually only one aircraft carrier is allowed. Ships cannot overlap on the grid: each series of squares denoting a ship must follow a straight line, either across the grid or vertically.

After the ships' positions have been marked on the grids, the first player calls out the location of a particular square, such as A-3, where his "shot" will land. If any of his opponent's ships, or part of a ship, occupies that square, then it takes a "hit" and has to be declared "Hit," and the square is filled in to signify the hit.

A player should record their own "shots called" by marking these on his "Enemy Ships" grid with a dot or similar mark, because this helps to prevent wasted "Missed" shots— any "Hits" that are called should also be marked with an X to give an aiming point for future shots. If the square is empty, the lucky player says "Missed." Game play alternates between players until one player has no ships, or parts of a ship, afloat. The game then ends and the player with ships still afloat wins the game.

My Ships

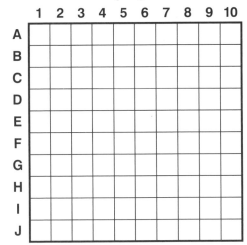

	1	2	3	4	5	6	7	8	9	10
A										
B										
C										
D										
E										
F										
G										
H										
I										
J										

Example game play

My Ships

	1	2	3	4	5
A				X	
B				X	
C					
D					

Enemy Ships

	1	2	3	4	5
A		•			
B	•		X	X	•
C			•		•
D					

Enemy Ships

	1	2	3	4	5	6	7	8	9	10
A										
B										
C										
D										
E										
F										
G										
H										
I										
J										

Rules:

Players must be honest with each other and declare "hits" in a truthful and sporting manner.

Pass Around the Drawing

3+   5-99   Medium

Pass Around the Drawing is a simple pencil and paper drawing game.

Game play:

The simplest form of this game is one where all of the players add a contribution to a group drawing. Place a clean sheet of paper on a clipboard or other hard surface. One person is chosen to start the game by drawing an item or object of their own choosing somewhere on the sheet of paper. This drawing should leave sufficient clear space on the paper to allow all of their fellow "artists" to have enough room to draw their chosen object to build up a picture.

As a suggestion, players could agree to draw one object from the scenery as the car passes it. The first player could draw a cow, the second a farm, the next an electricity pole, and so forth. This game lends itself to Alphabet Sketching where the first person does a drawing of an object beginning with "A," the next person adds an object beginning with "B," etc., (apple, boy, cow, duck ...)

Variation

This game can also be played where the artists take turns at nominating a character to be drawn in the manner described. This character could be a mermaid, a policeman, or any other that leaps from their imagination—the results could be very amusing.

Variation

Here is an old favorite—draw a part each. A piece of paper is folded evenly across its width five times, with each fold tucked behind the next, as if it had been rolled up then flattened. Starting at the open fold, the first player has to draw a hat, then folds the paper backward so that the next "artist" does not see what has been drawn. Passing the folded sheet to the next player, that person has to draw a head, then fold the paper backward for the following persons to add the body and arms (don't forget to add clothes!), the legs, and finally the feet (with or without shoes or boots) in the same way, and folding the sheet after each turn. Each artist can decide whether their part of the drawing is that of a male or female person, either an adult or a child—anything goes. When it is finished, pass the drawing around for all to admire the work of the other artists!

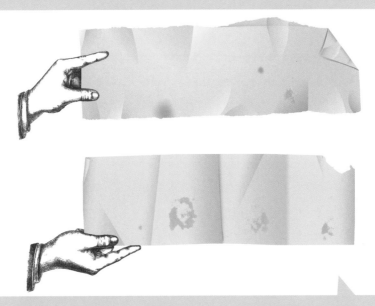

Variation

Another fun game for two players is called **Draw from my Squiggle**. In this game, one person draws a squiggle—without lifting the pencil from the paper. They then pass it to the other player, who tries to convert the squiggle into a drawing. This drawing can be that of a face, an animal, or anything. When the drawing is finished, the player who did the squiggle has to try to guess what the drawing represents. Try rotating the paper to help you visualize your drawing!

Guess What I'm Drawing

2+ | 5-99 | Medium

Guess What I'm Drawing is a game where players have to draw clues on a piece of paper for others to guess what the object might be.

Game play:

The player chosen to start the game thinks of an object. They then begin to draw a sketch that is only a small part of that object but only in sufficient detail to give a clue to the identity of that object. If none of the players can guess what the object is, the artist draws a little more of the object to give an extra clue as to its identity. If it is still not guessed correctly, another small part is added, and so forth until there is a correct guess. The winner of the game chooses the next object to be guessed, and draws a small part of that object as a clue, with the game progressing as before.

With a little skill and cunning, the artist can disguise the item being drawn by breaking it down in their imagination and only show various different parts of the object, ideally by drawing only unconnected parts in their series of "clue sketches." Even a simple outline of an object can be disguised in this way: for example, if the object is a fish, then the artist could draw a part of its outline, say a dorsal fin, then follow that with a part of its tail, or a gill flap, and so forth until somebody is able to mentally join the parts to guess that it is a fish. Try simple shapes at first, then make things harder as artistic disguises improve.

1

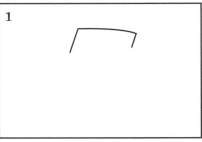

2

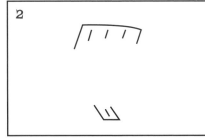

3

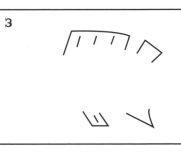

4

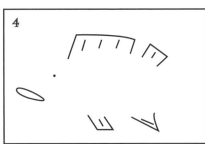

5

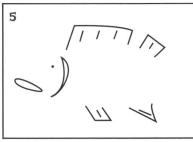

6

7

Rules:

The objects to be drawn should be only line drawings—no shading or solid blocks of pencil are allowed, because this could make the objects almost impossible to identify, as well as take longer to draw!

A candle.

131

GENERAL KNOWLEDGE AND TRIVIA

Countries of the World

1+   10-99   Medium to Hard

Can you identify the country by its flag?

(Answers at the end of the book on page 155.)

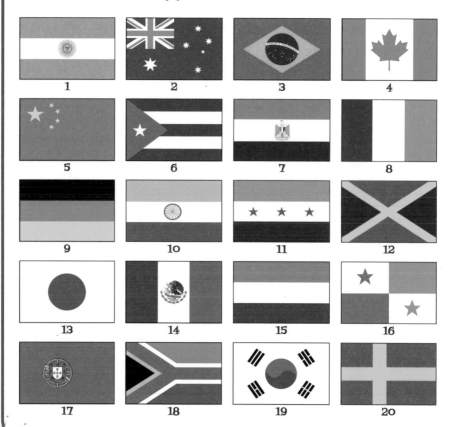

1   2   3   4

5   6   7   8

9   10   11   12

13   14   15   16

17   18   19   20

People and Populations

1+	10-99	Medium to Hard

1. A refugee is someone who:
    a.   has been forced to leave an area.
    b.   comes to a new country to find fame and fortune.
    c.   settles in a region other than where they were born.

2. People who come into a new country to live are:
    a.   emigrants   b.   immigrants

3. Population is fairly evenly distributed all over the earth.
    a.   True   b.   False

4. Most of the people in the world all live on a small proportion of the earth's surface.
    a.   True   b.   False

5. Which area has the least population density?
    a.   South and East Asia   b.   Eastern North America
    c.   Europe   d.   Northern Africa

6. Urban relates to:
    a.   the city   b.   the country

7. Characteristics of population include such things as language, religion, and customs.
    a.   True
    b.   False

(Answers can be found at the back of the book on page 155.)

Animals

1+   10-99   Medium to Hard

Write down the answers then check how many you got right.
(Answers at the end of the book on page 155.)

1. What food makes up nearly all (around 99 percent) of a Giant Panda's diet?

2. True or false? Mice live for up to 10 years.

3. What is the name of the phobia that involves an abnormal fear of spiders?

4. What is the largest type of "big cat" in the world?

5. True or false? Crocodiles have no sweat glands so they use their mouths to release heat.

6. Eagles are very good at spotting potential prey from a long distance. Why?

7. What are female elephants called?

8. True or false? Owls can turn their heads completely backward, allowing a 360-degree view.

9. Bees are found on every continent of the earth except for one. Which is it?

10. True or false? Cats spend an average of 13 to 14 hours a day sleeping.

11. What is the fastest land animal in the world?

12. A "doe" is what kind of animal?

13. True or false? Cougars are herbivores.

14. Groups of lions are known as what?

15. Is a dolphin a mammal?

Space and Planets

| 1+ | 10-99 | Medium to Hard |

How much do you know about planets, stars, moons, astronauts, our solar system, and the galaxy? (Check your answers to these questions against those given at the end of the book on page 155.)

1. What is the closest planet to the sun?

2. What is the name of the second biggest planet in our solar system?

3. What is the hottest planet in our solar system?

4. What planet is famous for its big red spot?

5. What planet is famous for the beautiful rings that surround it?

6. Can humans breathe normally in space as they can on Earth?

7. Is the sun a star or a planet?

8. Who was the first person to walk on the moon?

9. What planet is known as the red planet?

10. What is the name of the force holding us on Earth?

11. Have human beings ever set foot on Mars?

12. What is the name of a place that uses telescopes and other scientific equipment to research space and astronomy?

13. What is the name of NASA's most famous space telescope?

14. Earth is located in which galaxy?

Hot or Cold?

1+   10-99   Medium to Hard

Find out if you have paid enough attention to what you were told (or found out) in science class. (The correct answers are at the back of the book on page 155.)

1. True or false? The boiling point of water is 212°F.

2. When water is cooled, does it expand or contract?

3. True or false? The highest temperature ever recorded on the earth is 108.3°F.

4. Does heat from the sun get to the earth by radiation, conduction, or convention?

5. What is the freezing temperature of water?

6. True or false? Kelvin, Celsius, and Fahrenheit are all measures of temperature.

7. True or false? 100 degrees Kelvin is the temperature of absolute zero.

8. Substances that don't conduct heat are known as what?

9. True or false? Heat is a form of energy.

10. At what temperature is Fahrenheit equal to Celsius?

11. What instrument is used to measure temperature? a. barometer b. thermometer c. anemometer

12. What is the normal body temperature of a healthy, resting adult human being?

13. What is the highest shade temperature ever recorded on the surface of the earth?

14. What is the coldest temperature ever recorded on the earth?

Dogs

| | | 1+ | 10-99 | Medium to Hard |

Dogs are cute and playful when they are puppies and they soon become obedient(?) pets that are a joy to live with. These animals are wonderful companions. How much do you know about them? Try to answer these questions to see if you really do know about dogs. (Answers are at the back of the book on page 156.)

1. Is the domestic dog a carnivore, omnivore, or herbivore?

2. True or false? Like most mammals, dogs have color vision, which is similar to red-green color blindness in humans.

3. What is a dog's most powerful sense?

4. Is the average lifespan of dogs around 5 to 8 years, 10 to 13 years, or 15 to 18 years?

5. What is the most popular dog breed found in the United States?

6. True or false? Dogs are susceptible to parasites, such as ticks, mites, and fleas.

7. Who has better hearing: a human or a dog?

8. What is the name of the phobia for someone who has a fear of dogs?

9. True or false? The tallest dog in the world stands over 59 inches in height.

10. Because of dogs' unique relationship with humans, they are often referred to as man's best …?

11. What is the smallest breed of dog?

12. What is the tallest breed of dog?

Sports Science

1+   10-99   Medium to Hard

Good at sports? Think you know a lot about the subject? These questions are for you! (Answers are at the back of the book on page 156.)

1. Which decelerates faster: a badminton shuttlecock or a baseball?

2. True or false? Lower tension on a tennis racquet produces more control and less power.

3. In the Winter Olympic sport of curling, what type of rock are the curling stones made from?

4. True or false? Olympic gold medals contain more silver than gold.

5. How high is a regulation-size basketball hoop?

6. Does the chronic injury known as plantar fasciitis affect hands or feet?

7. True or false? Astronaut Alan Shepard hit a golf ball while on the moon in 1971.

8. What is typically the slowest swimming stroke: freestyle, backstroke, breaststroke, or butterfly?

9. True or false? The official distance of a marathon is 27.34 miles.

10. Does an injury to your anterior cruciate ligament affect your arm or leg?

11. True or false? Your body only produces lactic acid during intensive physical activity.

12. Do the fastest male 100-meter sprinters in the world average above or below 20 mph?

Tribes and Customs

1+   10-99   Medium to Hard

This is a fun quiz that will test your knowledge of our fellow dwellers on the planet Earth.
(The answers are at the back of the book on page 156, but try to get the questions before you look!)

1. What is the most commonly spoken language within the continent of Africa?

    a.   English   b.   French

    c.   Arabic   d.   Swahili

2. To which Native American tribe did Chief Sitting Bull belong?

    a.   Apache   b.   Dakota

    c.   Pawnee

3. Where do the Maori people live?

    a.   New Guinea   b.   Tonga

    c.   Australia   d.   New Zealand

4. Which modern-day country was the center of the Inca Empire in pre-Columbian South America?

    a.   Brazil   b.   Chile

    c.   Argentina   d.   Peru

5. Maypole dancing is a form of folk dance from:

    a.   England   b.   Sweden

    c.   Spain   d.   Portugal

    e.   Germany

Inventors and Inventions

1+	10-99	Medium to Hard

Who made the first ...? When was it? See if you know some of these. (Answers are at the back of the book on page 156.)

1. Who invented the reflecting telescope?

2. What year was Kevlar first marketed: 1969, 1971, or 1975?

3. In 1967, Christiaan Barnard performed the first: backward flip, heart transplant, or orbit around the moon?

4. Ladislao & Georg Biro invented the ballpoint pen in 1912, 1927, 1938, or 1952?

5. In 1967, Ralph Baer invented the first thermos, power boat, video game, or artificial eye?

6. The first coffee filter paper was invented in 1908 by James Starbuck, Alan Brazil, Melitta Bentz, or Ronald McDonald?

7. In 1923, the rapid dry-freezing of food was pioneered by Thomas Wall, Clarence Birdseye, Arthur Kellogg, or Ben and Jerry?

8. The first potato chips were invented by George Crum in which year: 1853, 1904, 1926, or 1949?

9. The first disposable razor was invented in 1901 by Brian Wilkinson, Edward Ronson, King Camp Gillette, or Sweeney Todd?

10. The ice cream soda was invented (and tasted!) by Robert Green in 1799, 1874, 1907, or 1914?

Roads and Vehicles

1+   10-99   Medium to Hard

You are on the road and traveling in a vehicle—how much do you know about the most common form of transport in the world? (Answers are at the back of the book on page 156.)

1. Who made the first road trip in a gas-engine motor vehicle in 1888: Henry Ford, Fred Talbot, Bertha Benz, or Austin Morris?

2. Approximately how far did they travel: 2 miles (3.2 kilometers), 13 miles (20.92 kilometers), 28 miles (45.06 kilometers), or 60 miles (96.56 kilometers)?

3. The first two-way carriageway road was opened in which country in 1921: England, Germany, Italy, or the United States?

4. Although private toll roads had existed since the 16th century, when was the first national toll road network established: 18th century, 19th century, or 20th century?

5. According to the Guinness Book of Records, which is the longest highway in the world: Route 66, the M6 motorway in England, Auto-route 1 in France, the Pan-American Highway, or the South African Trans-veldt track?

6. How long is the road in Question 5: 1,200 miles (1,931 kilometers), 3,967 miles (6,384 kilometers), 29,800 miles (47,958.45 kilometers), 958 miles (1,541 kilometers), or 649 miles (1,044 kilometers)?

7. Which make and model of car has been in production for the longest time: Aston Martin DB9, BMW Z3, Morgan 4/4, Volkswagen Beetle, or Fiat 600?

8. The longest production car of all time was the 1972-74 Cadillac Fleetwood 75. How long was it: 252.2 in, 197.7 in, or 288.3 in?

Food and its Origins

1+	10-99	Medium to Hard

How much do you really know about the food you eat? Take this fun food quiz and find out! (Answers are at the back of the book on page 156.)

1. The rice dish "paella" comes from what country?

2. Deer meat is known by what name?

3. What food is used as the base of guacamole?

4. The range of vegetables, fruits, meats, nuts, grains, herbs, and spices used in cooking are known as what?

5. True or false? India is the world's largest producer of bananas.

6. What is the sweet substance made by bees?

7. True or false? McDonald's has restaurants in over 100 countries around the world.

8. The "Pizza Hut" franchise began in what country?

9. Foods rich in starch, such as pasta and bread, are often known by what word starting with the letter C?

10. True or false? Trans fats are good for your health.

11. What is another name for maize?

12. Fruit preserves made from citrus fruits, sugar, and water are known as what?

Prehistoric Animals

1+   10-99   Medium to Hard

How much do you know about the creatures that lived on the earth millions of years ago—the dinosaurs? Which of these were herbivores and which were carnivores, and how many legs did they move on? (Try this very hard quiz—a pat on the back if you manage to get all of the answers correct—check at the back of the book on page 157.)

1. How many horns did triceratops have?

2. True or false? The name dinosaur means "terrible lizard."

3. Which came first, the Jurassic or Cretaceous Period?

4. Was diplodocus a carnivore or herbivore?

5. True or false? Tyrannosaurus rex was the biggest dinosaur ever.

6. True or false? Iguanodon was one of three dinosaurs that inspired the appearance of Godzilla.

7. Did theropods, such as allosaurus and carnotaurus, move on two legs or four?

8. Apatosaurus is also widely known by what other name?

9. True or false? Most dinosaurs became extinct during an event that occurred 500 years ago.

10. How long was the jaw bone of an adult Tyrannosaurus rex?

11. True or false? Dinosaur fossils have been found on every continent of the earth.

12. What dinosaur-themed book was turned into a blockbuster movie in 1993?

The Human Body

1+   10-99   Medium to Hard

How well do you know your own body? Find out by getting as many right answers to this quiz as you can. (Answers are at the end of the book on page 157.)

1. What is the name of the biggest part of the human brain?

2. The colored part of the human eye that controls how much light passes through the pupil is called the …?

3. What is the name of the substance that gives skin and hair its pigment?

4. The muscles found in the front of your thighs are known as what?

5. True or false? The two chambers at the bottom of your heart are called ventricles.

6. What substance are nails made of?

7. What is the human body's biggest organ?

8. The innermost part of bones contains what?

9. True or false? An adult human body has over 500 bones.

10. How many lungs does the human body have?

11. Another name for your voice box is the?

12. The two holes in your nose are called?

13. Your tongue is home to special structures that allow you to experience tastes such as sour, sweet, bitter, and salty. What is their name?

14. The bones that make up your spine are called what?

15. The shape of DNA is known as?

Math and Numbers

1+	10-99	Medium to Hard

Put your knowledge of math, geometry, and numbers to the test. How many of the questions can you answer correctly? (When you've finished simply turn to the end of the book to find out on page 157.)

1. What is the next prime number after 7?

2. The perimeter of a circle is also known as what?

3. 65-43 = ?

4. True or false? A convex shape curves outward.

5. What does the square root of 144 equal?

6. True or false? Pi can be correctly written as a fraction.

7. What comes after a million, billion, and trillion?

8. 52 divided by 4 equals what?

9. What is the bigger number, a googol or a billion?

10. True or false? Opposite angles of a parallelogram are equal.

11. 87 + 56 = ?

12. How many sides does a nonagon have?

13. True or false? -2 is an integer.

14. What is the next number in the Fibonacci sequence: 0, 1, 1, 2, 3, 5, 8, 13, 21, 34, ?

Metals and Elements

1+   10-99   Medium to Hard

Put yourself to the test with this fun science challenge and see how much general knowledge you have on metals. (Find out how you did at the back of the book on page 157.)

1. What is the chemical symbol of gold?

2. True or false? Steel is a chemical element.

3. What is the most common metal found on earth?

4. True or False? Sodium is a very reactive metal.

5. What three kinds of medals are awarded at the Olympic Games?

6. True or false? Metal bonding with metal is known as a metallic bond.

7. Bronze is made from what two metals?

8. What is the only metal that is liquid at room temperature?

9. True or false? Sterling silver is made up of less than 50 percent silver by weight.

10. What metal has the chemical symbol Pb?

11. What is the most abundant element in the universe?

12. What is the hardest metal on the earth?

13. What are generally accepted to be the eight "noble" metals?

14. Name two elements that are liquid at room temperature.

15. Dry ice is the solid form of which gas?

Highest Mountains

1+   10-99   Medium to Hard

1. Did you know that the 100 highest mountain peaks in the world are located in central and southern Asia? Maybe not.

   However, almost everybody knows that Mount Everest at 29,029 feet is the highest mountain in the world, but do you know which is the highest mountain in these places?

   a.   Europe   b.   Africa

   c.   South America   d.   Australia

   e.   North America

2. Which volcanic mountain erupted and buried Pompeii in 79 AD?

3. Which is the highest mountain in Japan?

4. On which continent are the Atlas mountains located?

5. Which mountain range is on the border between Europe and Asia?

6. Which mountain range passes through Venezuela, Colombia, Ecuador, Peru, Bolivia, Chile, and Argentina?

(Some of these are very difficult—if you get stuck (or give up!), look at the answers at the back of the book on page 157.)

Kids Jokes and Silly Stuff

1+   10-99   Medium to Hard

A is for Ants:

Where do ants go for their vacation? Frants!

What do you call an ant who skips school? A tru-ant!

What do you get if you cross some ants with some tics? All kinds of antics!

What do you call a greedy ant? An ant-eater!

What is even bigger than an elephant? A gi-ant!

E is for Elephants

What time is it when an elephant sits on the fence? Time to fix the fence!

What's gray, stands in a river when it rains, and doesn't get wet? An elephant with an umbrella!

What's gray with red spots? An elephant with the measles!

Why does an elephant wear slippers? So that he can sneak up on mice!

What's big and gray and wears a mask? The elephant-om of the opera!

Q: What did the judge say when the skunk walked in the courtroom? Odor in the court.

Q: What has no beginning, no end, and nothing in the middle? A doughnut!

Q: What has four wheels and flies? A garbage truck.

Q: What washes up on small beaches? Microwaves.

Q: Why shouldn't you take a bear to the zoo? Because they'd rather go to the movies!

Q: Which fruit gave its name to a desktop computer in 1984? Apple.

Q: What was the favorite food of the Teenage Mutant Ninja Turtles? Pizza.

Trivia:

The sentence "the quick brown fox jumps over the lazy dog" uses every letter in the English language.

The shortest war in history was between Zanzibar and England in 1896. Zanzibar surrendered after 38 minutes.

Check this out without them knowing: Women blink nearly twice as much as men.

If you can remember it, the word "lethologica" describes the state of not being able to remember the word you want.

The words RACECAR and KAYAK are palindromes. They are the same whether they are read left to right or, right to left.

TYPEWRITER is the longest word that can be made using the letters on only one row of the keyboard.

Cats have over 100 vocal sounds; dogs only have about 10.

Label on children's cough medicine: May cause drowsiness. Do not drive or operate machinery.

And finally:

FINISHED FILES ARE THE RESULT OF YEARS OF SCIENTIFIC STUDY COMBINED WITH THE EXPERIENCE OF YEARS.

Now count aloud the "F's" in that sentence. Count them **only once**; do not go back and count them again. How many letter "F's" did you count?

The answer is six: A person of average intelligence finds three of them. If you spotted four, you're above average. If you got five, you can turn up your nose at almost everybody. If you counted six, you are a genius. There is no catch. Many people miss those in the word "of." The human brain tends to see them as "V's" instead of "F's."

Invent Your Own Games

1+   10-99   Medium

Why not invent some games for yourself?

Hopefully, some of the games in this book may have amused and entertained the younger ones in the vehicle and helped to pass the time. Many of the games are traditional favorites, but there is always room for a new version or variation of an existing game.

Perhaps your family have already tried their own method of game play or have modified the rules to suit their own circumstances? In that case, they may be ready to try to create some games for themselves.

The game categories used in this book can form a starting point for deciding which type of game could be invented. Because there is unlikely to be a source of reference material within the car (apart from Mom or Dad!), this factor will largely exclude quizzes and trivia—unless you know better! It is much better to stick to the basics and not try anything too complicated at first—those can come later.

The types of games that simply rely on the powers of observation of those taking part tend to be the ones most people find satisfying. Basic counting games are surprisingly popular with younger children who want to show their command of numbers, as are those games that combine numbers with colors.

Observation game ideas can be inspired by the scenery outside the car. Just looking at the scenery can help: if you are traveling across a vast expanse of open countryside, it is unlikely that objects normally seen in a busy street will be spotted.

In this situation, animals, farms, and other rural objects will be more commonly seen.

The ages of those trying to invent a game will have to be taken into account as the needs and imagination of a five-year-old child will be much different from those of an older age group.

The older group will probably be more interested in devising games that require paper and pencil. There is plenty of scope for imaginative words or numbers games; the difficult part is trying to invent a game that hasn't been played before—at least, not by those in the car! Ideas for games that involve words or letters, or numbers and grids keep the mind occupied—which is part of the idea in the first place!

From simple word games to crossword-style word games, there are many variations to be discovered. Strategy games played on grids drawn on paper offer a whole range of possibilities. Just let their imaginations run free!

Word Scramble Solutions

Game 1:
a) BLUE b) ORANGE c) YELLOW d) PURPLE e) GREEN f) PINK g) BROWN
h) BLACK i) INDIGO j) WHITE

Game 2:
a) COW b) GOAT c) SHEEP d) ANTELOPE e) ELEPHANT f) TIGER g) SHARK
h) POLAR BEAR i) LEOPARD j) LYNX

Game 3:
a) ELIJAH b) GEORGE c) MARTIN d) PAMELA e) DEBBIE f) MADELEINE
g) CHRISTINE h) KEELEY i) AMANDA k) DONALD

Game 4:
a) TULIP b) DAISY c) HYACINTH d) DAFFODIL e) ORCHID
f) CHRYSANTHEMUM g) VIOLET h) ROSE i) CAMELIA k) BUTTERCUP

Game 5:
a) NEW YORK b) SYDNEY c) BERLIN d) ROME e) MUMBAI f) SAO PAOLO
g) JOHANNESBURG h) ANKARA i) WELLINGTON j) ACCRA

Game 6:
a) TENNIS b) SOCCER c) CRICKET d) GOLF e) HOCKEY f) BASEBALL g) RUGBY
h) ATHLETICS i) SKATING j) CYCLING

Quiz Answers

Average Speed Game:

1.   3 hours (135 miles ÷ 45 mph = 3 hours)
2.   52 miles (8 mph x 6.5 hours = 52 miles)
3a.   54 mph (216 miles ÷ 4 hours = 54 mph)
3b.   6.5 hours (351 miles ÷ 54 mph = 6.5 hours)
4.   3 hours (45 miles ÷ 15 mph = 3 hours)
5.   10 miles (4 mph x 2.5 hours = 10 miles)
6.   60 mph (300 miles ÷ 5 hours = 60 mph)
7.   63 miles (1.5 hours x 42 mph = 63 miles)
8.   5.5 hours (385 miles ÷ 70 mph = 5.5 hours)

Countries of the World:
1. Argentina 2. Australia 3. Brazil 4. Canada 5. China 6. Cuba 7. Egypt 8. France
9. Germany 10. India 11. Iraq 12. Jamaica 13. Japan 14. Mexico 15. The Netherlands
16. Panama 17. Portugal 18. South Africa 19. South Korea 20. Sweden

----

People and Populations:
1. a 2. b 3. b 4. a 5. d 6. a 7. a

Animals:
1. Bamboo 2. False—Captive mice live for up to two-and-a-half years while wild mice live for only
an average of around four months 3. Arachnophobia 4. The tiger, weighing up to 660 pounds
5. True—They often sleep with their mouth open to cool down 6. Because they have excellent
eyesight 7. Cows 8. False—Their field of view is about 270 degrees 9. Antarctica 10. True 11. The
cheetah—it can reach speeds of up to 75 mph 12. A female deer 13. False—They are carnivores
14. Prides 15. Yes

Space and Planets:
1. Mercury 2. Saturn 3. Venus 4. Jupiter 5. Saturn 6. No 7. A star 8. Neil Armstrong
9. Mars 10. Gravity 11. No 12. An observatory 13. Hubble Space Telescope
14. The Milky Way Galaxy

Hot or Cold?:
1. True 2. Expand 3. False, 136°F 4. Radiation 5. 32°F 6. True 7. False, 0°K (Kelvin)
8. Insulators 9. True 10. -40°F 11. Thermometer 12. 98.6°F 13. 136°F at Al Aziziyah, Libya
in 1922 14. -128.6°F at Vostock Station, Antarctica in 1983

Dogs:

1. Omnivore—Dogs can healthily eat a range of foods including grains and vegetables as part of their daily nutritional requirements without the need to solely rely on meat 2. True 3. Its sense of smell 4. 10 to 13 years 5. The Labrador Retriever 6. True 7. A dog—Dogs can hear both above and below humans on the frequency spectrum, can pinpoint sound direction much faster, and they can hear sounds that are four times as far away compared to the sounds that humans can hear 8. Cynophobia 9. False—The tallest dog is a Great Dane that stands 42.2 inches measured at the top of the shoulder 10. Friend 11. Chihuahua 12. Great Dane

----

Sports Science:

1. Shuttlecock 2. False (less control, more power) 3. Granite 4. True 5. 10 feet
6. Feet 7. True 8. Breaststroke 9. False—26.219 miles 10. Leg
11. False (it's produced all the time) 12. Above—around 22.37 mph

----

Tribes and Customs:

1. c 2. b 3. d 4. d 5. All of them!

Inventors and Inventions:

1. Isaac Newton, 1668 2. 1971 3. Heart transplant 4. 1938 5. Video game 6. Melitta Bentz
7. Clarence Birdseye 8. 1853 9. King Camp Gillette 10. 1874

Roads and Vehicles:

1. Bertha Benz 2. 60 miles (96.56 kilometers) 3. Italy 4. 18th century 5. Pan-American Highway
6. 29,800 miles (47,958.45 kilometers) 7. Morgan 4/4 from 1936 to present 8. 252.2 inches

----

Food and its Origins:

1. Spain 2. Venison 3. Avocado 4. Ingredients 5. True 6. Honey 7. True 8. The United States
9. Carbohydrates 10. False 11. Corn 12. Marmalade

Prehistoric Animals:

1. Three 2. True 3. The Jurassic Period 4. Herbivore 5. False 6. True 7. Two 8. Brontosaurus
9. False (65 million years ago) 10. 4 feet (1.2 m) 11. True 12. Jurassic Park

----

The Human Body:

1. The cerebrum 2. Iris 3. Melanin 4. Quadriceps 5. True 6. Keratin 7. The skin
8. Bone marrow 9. False (there are 206) 10. Two 11. Larynx 12. Nostrils
13. Taste buds 14. Vertebrae 15. A double helix

Math and Numbers:

1. 11 2. The circumference 3. 22 4. True 5. 12 6. False 7. A quadrillion 8. 13
9. A googol 10. True 11. 143 12. 9 13. True 14. 55

Metals and Elements:

1. Au 2. False—Alloy 3. Iron 4. True 5. Gold, silver, and bronze 6. True 7. Copper and tin
8. Mercury 9. False—Over 92% 10. Lead 11. Hydrogen 12. Alloy 1090, a high-carbon steel
13. Ruthenium, rhodium, palladium, silver, osmium, iridium, platinum, and gold 14. Bromine and
mercury 15. Carbon dioxide

Highest Mountains:

1. (a.) Mont Blanc 15,774 feet, France-Italy border (b.) Mount Kilimanjaro 19,340.5 feet, in
Tanzania (c.) Aconcagua 22,841 feet, Andes Range, Argentina (d.) Mount Kosciuszko 7,310 feet,
Great Dividing Range, New South Wales (e.) Mount McKinley, 20,320 feet, in Alaska 2. Mount
Vesuvius 3. Mount Fuji 4. Africa 5. Urals 6. Andes.

What Time Did We Arrive?

1+   10-99

You have finally arrived at your destination!
Good job!

Just one more thing to do with that paper and pencil:

Write down your time of arrival!
In case you have forgotten, some of the players may have been playing the Average Speed Game. To complete this game, they will need to know the arrival time to be able to calculate how long the trip has taken—perhaps allowing for any stops on the way— or the others in the group may want to know just for general interest.

Because you are all excited at having reached your vacation destination, or that visit to grandma's house, you will be too busy to bother with those calculations right now— but if you write down the time now, you can always work it all out on the way home!

Wheel Lottery: We're There— Let's Find Out Who Has Won!

2+	1-99	Easy

This game is a favorite with airmen who use it to find out who buys the first drinks after a flight, or as a lottery wheel to decide the winner of a sweepstake. If a line is exactly at the bottom, a tie is declared. It is a simple but fun game that adds just a little more interest at the end of the trip. Good luck!

Winning position when stopped

Credits

The author would like to thank her four children and seven grandchildren for the experiences we had together over many years of car travel. Most of the games and pastimes in this book have been rigorously tested by them.—J.A.

Images courtesy of Shutterstock with the exception of pages 111, 115, 117, and 129 supplied by iStockphoto. Pages 25 and 129 supplied by KG and MG.